SKILL-STREAM-ING THE ELEMEN-TARY SCHOOL CHILD

A GUIDE FOR TEACHING PROSOCIAL SKILLS

Ellen McGinnis & Arnold P. Goldstein
with Robert P. Sprafkin & N. Jane Gershaw

RESEARCH PRESS COMPANY
2612 North Mattis Avenue
Champaign, Illinois 61821

Advisory Editor, Frederick H. Kanfer

Cover design by Jack Davis
Illustrations by Jane Caraway

Copies of this book may be ordered from the publisher at the address given on the title page.

ISBN 0-87822-235-9

Library of Congress Catalog Card Number 84-61282

15 14 13 12 11 10 9   95 96 97

To Sara, for the joy and love you bring to this world.

And to a richer, fuller life for all special needs children—
behaviorally disordered, learning disabled, mentally handicapped, and others.

Contents

Acknowledgments

Very special thanks must go to Laurie Sauerbry, who implemented much of this material in her classroom and who enthusiastically supported Structured Learning for elementary school children; to Polly Nichols for providing both a personal and professional model to emulate; to Carl Smith, whose active commitment to improve the education of behaviorally disordered children in Iowa has made this endeavor possible; to Beth Dorsey for her thoughtful suggestions, encouragement, and review of this manuscript; and to Jane Caraway, who supplied the warm and lively illustrations of children.

CHAPTER 1

Introduction

At recess several third graders were involved in a game of kickball, while Todd walked by himself on the outskirts of the playing field. When approached by the playground supervisor and asked why he didn't join in the game, Todd just shrugged his shoulders and walked away. He usually spends his recess time wandering around the playground alone or sitting in the school building entryway waiting for recess to be over.

In another school, while the sixth graders were working on their math assignments, a student passed by Michelle's desk and accidentally knocked her math assignment to the floor. Michelle jumped from her seat and held her fist in front of the student's face. "You did that on purpose! I'll get you for it!" Michelle yelled as she pushed the girl away from her. The classroom teacher then intervened.

And in yet a different school, as Brian walked through the hallway to his classroom, a group of fourth graders began taunting him. "Stop it! Stop it!" Brian shouted back. As the group continued to tease him, Brian ran into the classroom. Amidst tears, he begged his teacher to "make them stop."

Situations such as these are encountered by most teachers of elementary-age students. Children who repeatedly deal with daily events in an immature manner, with aggressiveness, or with withdrawal account for the majority of children described as behavior disordered (Quay, 1979). Even for those children who exhibit these behaviors less chronically, such behaviors may still interfere with the development of their personal happiness and satisfying relationships with others.

1

   While the public has, for the most part, traditionally taken the position that the primary role of the schools is to teach children the three Rs, teachers are increasingly assuming greater responsibility for teaching appropriate social and behavioral skills to their students. Many teachers of elementary-age students have expressed concern and even frustration regarding the disruptive, withdrawing, or otherwise problematic behavior of some of the children in their classrooms and their increasing difficulty in trying to deal constructively with such behaviors. We have often heard such questions as: Why do so many of my students show disrespect to their fellow students and to their teachers? When students misbehave, they know what the consequences will be . . . why don't they change? I have a student in my class who is ostracized by everyone, and I can certainly understand why . . . but what can I do for a child like this?

   Many teachers in today's school systems find themselves spending much of their time dealing with playground conflict, hallway and cafeteria disruptions, off-task behavior within the classroom itself, and much more. Many educators are concluding that the time spent trying to deal with these behavior problems can be better employed in teaching children how to prevent conflicts or deal with them in an effective, socially acceptable manner. The field of special education, in particular, is beginning to recognize the importance of providing students with instruction in problem-reducing and problem-avoiding prosocial and affective skills and competencies. The need for such instruction arises from the Education For All Handicapped Children Act of 1975 (P.L. 94-142) (Federal Register, 1975), which mandated that handicapped children be educated in the least restrictive environment.

> To the maximum extent appropriate, handicapped children, including children in public or private institutions or other care facilities, are educated with children who are not handicapped . . . and separate classes, separate schooling or other removal of handicapped children from the regular educational environment occurs only when the nature or severity of the handicap is such that education in regular classes . . . cannot be achieved satisfactorily. (Federal Register, Public Law 94-142, Education for All Handicapped Children Act of 1975, p. 17)

With the enactment of this mandate, special educators have focused on increasing the academic skills of handicapped children in preparation for mainstream placement and effective academic functioning in the least restrictive school setting. However, even when such academic goals have been realized, attempts at integrating handicapped children with their non-handicapped peers have often failed. Mainstreaming handicapped children into regular education classes and school social settings does not insure peer acceptance; in fact, the opposite quite often appears to be the case. Several studies indicate that handicapped children interact less, and in more reciprocally negative ways, with their peers than do nonhandicapped children (Allen, Benning, & Drummond, 1972; Bryan & Bryan, 1978; Bryan, Wheeler, Felcan, & Henek, 1976; Strain, Shores, & Timm, 1977). One means for substantially improving the likelihood that successful mainstreaming will be achieved is to provide instruction in prosocial skills to handicapped children.

Why do children, whether or not their behaviors are chronic or intense enough to be considered handicapped, often respond to others in problematic and self-defeating ways? Clearly, children with such problems have *too much* of a given behavior—withdrawal, aggression, or immaturity. Many educational interventions are available that concentrate on decreasing such inappropriate or undesirable behaviors. However, while such children possess too much of certain problematic behaviors, they also do not have *enough* of other behaviors, the prosocial ones, in their repertoires. These children lack, or are weak in, the skills, abilities, or behaviors needed to be socially competent. In other words, such students are deficient in prosocial skills just as low achievers are deficient in academic skills. Such deficits require direct and planned teaching. Morse (1982) states: "There are those who would admonish or exhort their pupils 'to behave' rather than teach them how to relate positively to each other. Seldom would we admonish a pupil to read in place of teaching the necessary skills" (p. 209). Thus, it is not enough merely to tell a student that an action is not acceptable; additional measures must be taken to *teach* the student *what to do*, as well as what not to do. The goal of this book is to provide teachers and others with a well-validated technique designed to systematically teach children the behaviors necessary for effective and satisfying social interactions.

Why don't all children learn acceptable social behavior? Cox and Gunn (1980) point out three reasons why children may fail to respond appropriately in social situations: (1) the child may not know what the appropriate behavior is; (2) she may have the knowledge, but may lack the practice; or (3) her emotional responses may inhibit the performance of the desirable behavior. The child with insufficient knowledge of the desirable behavior may not have attended to the correct use (modeling) of the prosocial behavior by others, or such appropriate models may not have been available in the child's environment. It may also be the case that the child has attended to an appropriate model, and learned the desirable behaviors, but is unsure where and when to use (or not use) these behaviors. This type of skill failure can be referred to as a lack of behavioral flexibility—the inability to adjust one's behavior to a variety of different situations, people, and/or settings. For example, a student may know how to request help from a peer in a socially acceptable manner, but such a request, while acceptable during independent seatwork, is inappropriate during an individual testing situation or a class discussion.

Cox and Gunn's (1980) second explanation for student failure to learn needed prosocial skills is that the student may lack sufficient opportunity or motivation to practice the prosocial behaviors that constitute the skill. A common example of lack of practice is the child who is aware that "thank you" is a polite thing to say when someone does a favor for her; however, because of absence of reward from others for doing so, she rarely responds this way. In this case, the child has not practiced the skill enough for it to become a part of her functioning behavioral repertoire.

We also know that many times children can verbalize a variety of prosocial alternatives, but nevertheless fail to utilize them when it would be appropriate to do so. For example, although Michelle reacts with physical aggression when annoyed by a peer, it is quite possible that she would be able to state ways she could have dealt with such provocation in a nondestructive way (e.g., ignoring the student), but she just cannot seem to overtly react in this appropriate manner. The tendency on our part, then, is to assume that Michelle has learned the prosocial skill, and could have ignored the incident if she had wanted to. We must recognize, however, that verbalizing prosocial alternatives is very different from actually being able to carry them out.

Michelle's reaction is an example of emotional responses inhibiting the performance of socially acceptable behaviors, Cox and Gunn's (1980) third explanation for social inappropriateness. Emotions such as anxiety, fear, or anger may prevent the child from thinking and responding effectively. Todd, for example, may have observed other students asking to join in a recess activity, and therefore may know the appropriate manner in which to ask to join the group. However, his fear of not being accepted by the group or not being skilled enough at the activity may prevent him from making the attempt. In such cases, the child must not only become proficient in using a prosocial skill, but must also learn how to stop the impulse to react with the inhibiting, problematic pattern of behavior.

Another reason why children succumb to problematic behaviors prompted by emotion is that they may be reinforced for undesirable behaviors and not adequately reinforced for prosocial ones. For instance, a young child may get attention much more quickly by whining than by quietly expressing her wants. Likewise, it may be easy for a teacher to inadvertently ignore a young student's appropriate request for help, but who can ignore a full-blown temper tantrum?

Who should receive instruction in prosocial skills? The prosocial skills approach presented in this book is designed for use with handicapped and nonhandicapped students in the elementary grades. Since handicapped students (e.g., mentally handicapped, learning disabled, and behaviorally disordered children) have been found to interact with peers less frequently and in more negative ways than nonhandicapped students (Gresham, 1981), prosocial skills instruction should be a central part of their special education instruction. As noted earlier, the teaching of positive, productive social behaviors also may increase their chances for successful mainstreaming.

Instruction in prosocial skills is also needed for many handicapped and nonhandicapped students who already are educated in the mainstream environment. Research suggests that prosocial skills deficits in children are related to school maladjustment (Gronlund & Anderson, 1963), delinquency (Roff, Sells, & Golden, 1972), and peer rejection (Quay, 1979). Children with poor interpersonal skills, as compared to their socially competent peers, have also been found to be at high risk for adjustment problems in adulthood (Cowen, Pederson, Babigian, Izzo, & Trost, 1973).

For many students, prosocial skills deficits are not limited to the minor difficulties that can be remediated through incidental teaching, such as teacher–student discussions. Instead, direct and systematic teaching of specific behaviors is often required. We believe that teaching prosocial behavioral alternatives at an early age may enhance a child's personal development and may aid in the prevention of more serious difficulties in adolescence and early adulthood. Most generally, our view is that teaching prosocial skills, for both remediation and preventive purposes, is a valuable intervention for those handicapped and nonhandicapped children, mainstreamed or not, showing the kind of undesirable behaviors or skill deficits that result in personal unhappiness, interpersonal difficulty, or academic ineffectiveness.

Who should teach prosocial skills? This book provides teachers of mainstream and special education classes with both a guiding strategy and concrete techniques for group instruction in prosocial skills. Other appropriate users of prosocial skills training include resource teachers and school support personnel such as social workers, psychologists, and school counselors. Although the primary focus is on teaching in public school settings, counselors and teachers in mental health and residential facilities will also find this method appropriate and useful to their needs.

OVERVIEW

This book provides all the information necessary for planning and implementing prosocial skills instruction. Chapter 2 gives the reader a detailed description of the components of Structured Learning. Screening procedures to assist in identifying children who are deficient in prosocial skills and their specific skill strengths and weaknesses are presented in Chapter 3. Chapter 4 instructs teachers and others who wish to begin Structured Learning groups in specific methods for planning and organizing such groups with elementary-age children. Chapter 5 presents the reader with a step-by-step guide for the implementation of Structured Learning with young children. A full listing of prosocial skills and their behavioral steps, that is, the suggested Structured Learning curriculum for instruction, along with lesson plans and suggested application situations, are the focus of Chapter 6. An example of a Structured Learning session with skill-deficient children (Chapter 7), suggestions for enhancing social skills learning and integrating Structured Learning into the students' daily educational program (Chapter 8), and specific techniques for managing individual and group behavior problems (Chapter 9) are also presented.

A separate booklet, *Program Forms*, contains additional reproducible materials for use in this program. It includes all the forms that appear in this book in a large, 8½ x 11-inch format, plus additional, different versions of contracts, student self-monitoring forms, and award forms.*

SUMMARY

We believe that the teaching of prosocial skills should be a part of all mainstream and special education programs. We believe that teachers must not only make students aware of specific behaviors that are unacceptable, but must actually teach constructive behavioral alternatives as well. The approach presented in this book advocates the teaching of prosocial alternatives to children in a manner similar to the teaching of academic competencies—using planned and systematic applied psychoeducational techniques. Our goal is to instruct teachers of elementary-age children in doing just that through a method called Structured Learning (Goldstein, 1973, 1981; Goldstein, Sprafkin, & Gershaw, 1976; Goldstein, Sprafkin,

---

*Available from Research Press, P.O. Box 3177, Champaign, IL 61821.

Gershaw, & Klein, 1980). Structured Learning is a psycho-educational intervention designed to teach the skill-deficient child prosocial alternative behaviors and to facilitate the actual use of these alternatives. This technique has found widespread, successful use with handicapped and nonhandicapped children alike.

CHAPTER 2

Components of Structured Learning

Structured Learning is a psychoeducational, behavioral approach for providing instruction in prosocial skills. It consists of (1) modeling, (2) role playing, (3) performance feedback, and (4) transfer of training. Each skill to be taught is first broken down into its constituent parts or behavioral steps. Students are then shown examples of people (models) performing these behavioral steps in an expert manner. Next, the students rehearse or practice the skill steps they have observed (role playing), and receive feedback from other students and from the group's trainers. Such feedback often takes the form of approval or praise as the role-played behavior becomes more and more like that of the model (performance feedback). Finally, a number of procedures are utilized that enhance the likelihood of the students' using these newly learned skills in real-life situations (transfer of training). Each of these components will be discussed in detail in this chapter.

MODELING

Modeling, defined as learning by imitation, has been shown to be an effective teaching method for children and adolescents (Bandura, Ross, & Ross, 1961; Rogers-Warren & Baer, 1976; Rosenthal, 1976). Three types of learning by modeling have been identified.

1. *Observational learning* is the learning of new behaviors not previously in the child's behavioral repertoire. Children

often observe and imitate other children in the way they dress, talk, and behave. The use of new slang expressions, which filter through schools and neighborhoods, is one frequent example of observational learning.

2. *Inhibitory and disinhibitory effects* involve the strengthening or weakening of behavior performed only rarely by the child. The behavior may be strengthened or weakened according to whether others are observed to be rewarded or punished for it. Children may see another child go unpunished or even be rewarded for behaving rudely or aggressively, and then react in a similar manner (disinhibitory effect). Alternatively, children may inhibit these reactions when they observe aggressive behavior being punished (inhibitory effect). Peer modeling is a major source of inhibitory and disinhibitory effects, and it frequently results in children's succumbing to "peer pressure."

3. *Behavioral facilitation* refers to the performance of previously learned behaviors that are already within the child's behavioral repertoire and are positively received by others. For example, when a child buys something she seems to enjoy, a friend may then buy one too. Another example of this type of modeling is when one student deals successfully with a problem (e.g., an assignment which is not understood) and a classmate approaches the problem in a similar way.

Research has demonstrated that many behaviors can be learned, strengthened, weakened, or facilitated through modeling. These include helping others, behaving independently, acting aggressively, acting nonaggressively, exhibiting certain speech patterns, interacting socially, and many more. It is clear that modeling can be an effective way of teaching people new behaviors.

Yet it is also true that individuals observe a variety of behaviors that they do not then engage in themselves. For example, the television, radio, magazines, and newspapers present very polished modeling displays of people buying products, but not everyone then buys those products. Children may see dozens, even hundreds, of behaviors enacted by peers in a typical school day, but copy only a few, or none, in response.

Apparently, then, people learn by modeling under some circumstances but not others. Research on modeling has identified several conditions that increase the effectiveness of modeling. These modeling enhancers include characteristics of the model, the modeling display, or the person observing the modeling. Since, as will be seen in Chapter 5, much of the prosocial skill modeling done in a Structured Learning group is done live by the teacher, it is crucial that he have a keen understanding of events and model qualities that enhance the potency of the modeling process.

MODELING ENHANCERS

Model Characteristics

More effective modeling will occur when the model (1) seems to be highly skilled in the behavior; (2) is considered by the observer to be of high status; (3) is friendly and helpful; (4) is of the same age, sex, and social status as the observer; (5) controls rewards desired by the observer; and, of particular importance, (6) is rewarded for the behavior. In other words, we are all more likely to imitate powerful yet pleasant people who receive rewards for what they are doing, especially when the reward is something that we, too, desire.

Modeling Display Characteristics

More effective modeling will occur when the modeling display demonstrates the behaviors (1) in a clear and detailed manner; (2) in order from the least difficult to the most difficult; (3) with enough repetition to facilitate overlearning; (4) with little irrelevant detail; and (5) with several individuals serving as models.

Observer (Student) Characteristics

More effective modeling will occur when the person observing the model is (1) instructed to imitate the model; (2) friendly toward or likes the model; (3) similar in background to the model; and, especially important, (4) rewarded for performing the behaviors that have been modeled.

RESEARCH ON MODELING

Much research has been done on the effectiveness of modeling. In early studies, for example, modeling was used to enhance the self-disclosure of personal concerns within interview situations (Marlatt, Jacobson, Johnson, & Morrice, 1970), to increase interviewees' liking for the interviewers (Friedenberg, 1971; Walsh, 1971), to decrease anxiety about public speaking (Kleinsasser, 1968), and to reduce schoolchildren's fears about examinations (Mann, 1972). Indeed, a great deal of learning, both in everyday situations and in laboratory and school settings, can be attributed to the effects of modeling.

Modeling is particularly effective with children and adolescents. In a large number of studies, Bandura and his colleagues demonstrated that children do in fact exhibit more aggressive behaviors when vivid modeling displays of such behaviors are presented to them (Bandura, Ross, & Ross, 1961). Such observational learning of aggression by children is a frequently replicated research finding (Fairchild & Erwin, 1977; Kirkland & Thelen, 1977; Rosenthal, 1976). In addition to enhancing the observational learning of aggressive behavior, modeling has been used successfully with children to teach such prosocial behaviors as social affiliativeness (Evers & Schwarz, 1973), creativity (Zimmerman & Dialissi, 1973), self-control (Toner, Moore, & Ashley, 1978), sharing (Canale, 1977; Grusec, Kuczynski, Rushton, & Simutis, 1978; Rogers-Warren & Baer, 1976), certain cognitive skills (Lowe & Cuvo, 1976), and even imitation itself (Kaufman, Gordon, & Baker, 1978).

MODELING—NECESSARY BUT INSUFFICIENT

The positive outcome of modeling research indicates that modeling is a powerful teaching technique. If modeling is so effective, why then are the other Structured Learning components (role playing, performance feedback, and transfer of training) needed? The answer is clear: Modeling alone is not enough because its many positive effects are very often short-lived. For example, ministers who were taught through modeling to be more empathic when conducting interviews were more empathic immediately after training, but a very short time later their increased empathy had disappeared (Perry, 1970). A modeling study of empathy with nurses and hospital aides produced the same result (Sutton, 1970).

Learning appears to be improved when the learner has the opportunity and is encouraged to practice, rehearse, or role play the behaviors performed by the model, and when the learner is rewarded for doing so. In other words, viewing the modeling display teaches the child *what* to do. In addition, he needs enough practice to learn *how* to do it and sufficient reward to motivate him, or to let him know *why* he should behave in certain ways. Let us turn now to the *how* question—the second component of Structured Learning, role playing.

ROLE PLAYING

Role playing has been defined as "a situation in which an individual is asked to take a role (behave in certain ways) not normally his own, or if his own, in a place not normal for the enactment of the role" (Mann, 1956, p. 227). The use of role playing to help a person change his behavior or attitudes has been a popular approach in education for many years. Teachers of elementary school children frequently direct their students in role playing stories, plays, and problem occurrences to assist in developing comprehension and new behavioral skills.

ROLE-PLAY ENHANCERS

Research also impressively demonstrates the value of role playing for behavior and attitude change. However, as with modeling, behavior or attitude change through role playing will be more likely to occur if certain conditions are met. These role-play enhancers include (1) choice on the part of the student regarding whether to take part in the role playing; (2) the student's commitment to the behavior or attitude she is role playing, which is fostered by the public (rather than private) nature of the role play that makes it difficult for the child to disown; (3) improvisation in enacting the role-play behaviors; and (4) reward, approval, or reinforcement for enacting the role-play behaviors.

RESEARCH ON ROLE PLAYING

Perhaps as many as a hundred studies have been done, mostly directed at discovering the effects of role playing on attitude change. In the typical experiment of this type, the research subjects are first given some sort of attitude questionnaire and are then placed in one of three experimental groups. Those assigned to the role-playing group must actively defend a viewpoint (such as making a speech or other public statement) that is opposed to what they really believe. Subjects in the second group, the exposure group, hold the same private attitudes as the role-playing subjects but are not requested to make such a speech opposite to their real attitudes. They are simply required to listen to one of the speeches made by a role-playing subject. Control group subjects neither make nor hear such a speech. All subjects are then given the attitude questionnaire a second time. This type of experiment has consistently shown that role-playing subjects change in their attitudes (away from what they privately believed toward what they publicly said) significantly more than either exposure or control subjects.

Role players have shown significantly more behavior and attitude change than observers or controls on such dimensions as school attendance (Shoabs, 1964), social skills (Hubbel, 1954), acceptance of minority children (Nichols, 1954), interpersonal sensitivity in classroom settings (Chesler & Fox, 1966), attitudes toward another person (Davis & Jones, 1960), moral judgment (Arbuthnot, 1975; Mately & Acksen, 1976), conflict management skills (Spivak & Shure, 1974), altruism (Iannotti, 1977), empathy (Staub, 1971), and a variety of other prosocial skills (Ross, Ross, & Evans, 1976; Rathjen, Hiniker, & Rathjen, Note 1). Thus, it is clear that role playing can lead to many types of behavior and attitude change.

ROLE PLAYING—NECESSARY BUT INSUFFICIENT

As with modeling, role playing may be seen as a necessary but insufficient behavior change technique. Its effects, as when modeling is used alone, often do not last (Lichtenstein, Keutzer, & Himes, 1969). Thus, in most attempts to help a person change his behavior, neither modeling nor role playing alone is enough. Combining the two is an improvement, for then the student knows both what to do and how to do it. But even this combination is insufficient, for the child still needs to know *why* he should behave in new ways. That is, a motivational or incentive component must be added. It is for this reason that performance feedback, to be considered next, is the third component of Structured Learning.

PERFORMANCE FEEDBACK

Performance feedback is defined as providing the student with information on how well he has done during the role playing, particularly how well his enactment of the skill's behavioral steps corresponded to the model's expert portrayal of them. Feedback may take such forms as constructive suggestions for improvement, prompting, coaching, material reward, and especially such social reinforcement as praise and approval.

Reinforcement typically has been defined as any event that serves to increase the likelihood that a given behavior will occur. Three types of reinforcement have been described: (1) material reinforcement, such as food or money; (2) social reinforcement, such as praise or approval from others; and (3) self-reinforcement, which is a person's positive evaluation of his own behavior. Effective performance feedback must give attention to all three types of reinforcement. Material reinforcement may be viewed as a necessary base, without which the "higher" levels of reinforcement (social and self-reinforcement) may not function. For many young students, material reinforcement may be the only class of reinforcement to which they will respond initially. Because there is considerable evidence that behavior that has changed in response to a program of material rewards only typically disappears (extinguishes) when the rewards are no longer forthcoming, and because social rewards are more likely to be the type of reward available to the child outside of the training setting, an effort should be made to pair social reinforcers with the material reinforcer when providing positive performance feedback. The goal is subsequently to eliminate the material reinforcer while retaining the social reward. In other words, it is important that a teaching effort not rely too heavily or too long on material reinforcers, although they may be necessary in the beginning stages of work with handicapped or non-handicapped children.

Even though social reinforcers may be more available than material reinforcers in the real-life sense described before, it is also true that many valuable real-life behaviors go unnoticed, uncommented upon, and unappreciated by others. Therefore social reinforcement, too, may at times be an unreliable ally in the teaching process. Such potential social reinforcement suppliers as teachers, parents, and friends may often be either nonrewarding or simply unavailable. However, if students can be aided in becoming their own reinforcement suppliers, if they can be helped to evaluate their own skill behaviors and reward or approve their own effective performance, a major stride will have been made toward increasing the chances that newly learned skills will be performed in a reliable and lasting manner in real-life settings. Clearly, this is the goal of any reinforcement program. However, until the student has the skills to accurately evaluate his own performance, and has the self-confidence to do so, others in his environment (teachers, parents, peers) must be the reinforcement providers.

REINFORCEMENT ENHANCERS

The effectiveness of reinforcement in influencing performance will depend on several characteristics of the reinforcement used. These characteristics, or reinforcement enhancers, include the following.

Type of Reinforcement

McGehee and Thayer (1961) have observed: "What one person regards as a rewarding experience may be regarded by another as neutral or nonrewarding, or even punishing" (p. 140). While it is true that certain types of reinforcers, such as approval, food, affection, and money, have a high likelihood of serving as effective reinforcers for most people most of the time, this will not always be the case. Both the individual's own reinforcement history and current needs will affect whether the intended reinforcer is, in fact, reinforcing. Teaching procedures will optimally take these individualizing consider-ations into account. This means not only choosing between given material, social, and self-reinforcers when necessary, but also making changes in these choices in a continuing and sensitive manner.

Delay of Reinforcement

Research on learning has shown consistently that behavior change occurs most effectively when the reinforcement follows immediately after the desired behavior. Reinforcement strengthens the behavior that was occurring just before the reinforcement took place and makes it likely that that particular behavior will occur again. Thus, delayed reinforcement may lead to the strengthening of inappropriate or ineffective behaviors if these behaviors occur between the desired behavior and the onset of reinforcement.

Response-Contingent Reinforcement

It is necessary that students see and understand a relationship between the behavior they are exhibiting and the reinforcement that occurs. Delivering the reinforcement conditionally upon the behavior, and further making it sufficiently clear to the student that the reinforcement is contingent upon *this* selected behavior, is vital in creating the linkage between performance and reinforcement.

Amount and Quality of Reinforcement

The amount and quality of reinforcement also determine a student's performance. With certain important exceptions, the greater the amount of reinforcement, the greater the positive effect upon performance. One limitation on this principle is that increases in certain types of reinforcement do increase performance, but in smaller and smaller increments. Research on the amount of reinforcement indicates that, in the laboratory at least, subjects do not appear to learn (acquire new knowledge) more rapidly for large rewards than for small ones. Once learning has taken place, however, performance will often be more dependable if larger rewards are given.

Opportunity for Reinforcement

An additional requirement for successful and consistent performance is that the behavior to be reinforced occur with sufficient frequency for reinforcement to be provided often enough. If such behaviors are too infrequent, insufficient opportunity will exist to influence their occurrence through contingent reinforcement. Role playing provides excellent opportunities to reinforce the behaviors desired.

Partial (Intermittent) Reinforcement

Partial reinforcement refers to the reinforcement of only some of the person's correct responses by reinforcing at fixed times (e.g., at the end of each class period), at a fixed number of responses (e.g., every third correct response), on a variable time or response schedule (e.g., randomly choosing, within limits, the time or correct response to reward), and on other types of schedules. In all instances it has been consistently shown that behaviors that have been intermittently reinforced are longer lasting than behaviors reinforced each time they occur. An optimal reinforcement schedule provides rewards for all desired responses initially, thinning to one or another partial reinforcement schedule as the desired behavior continues.

In summary of performance feedback by reinforcement: (1) The reinforcement must be seen as rewarding by the child; (2) the reinforcement should be given immediately after the desired behavior; (3) the child must make the connection between the behavior she exhibits and the reinforcement she receives; (4) in general, the greater the amount of reinforcement, the greater the positive effect on performance; (5) the desirable behavior must occur sufficiently frequently for the reinforcement to be provided often enough; and (6) reinforcement should be given on a rich schedule at first, then thinned to an intermittent schedule. In other words, research evidence indicates that high levels of performance are likely to occur if the students are given enough opportunity to receive immediate reinforcement of a kind that is right for them, in sufficiently large amounts, offered in a response-contingent manner on an intermittent schedule.

REINFORCEMENT—NECESSARY, BUT INSUFFICIENT

There is considerable evidence supporting the impact on behavior change of modeling, role playing, and performance feedback in the form of social reinforcement. We have held that neither modeling alone nor role playing alone yields results nearly as effective as the two combined. We now wish to take a similar position regarding reinforcement. While it is true that reinforcement alone is more likely to lead to lasting behavior change than either modeling or role playing alone, it is also true that the behaviors to be reinforced must occur with sufficient correctness and sufficient frequency for reinforcement to have its intended effect. The addition of modeling increases the likelihood that the behavior to be reinforced will be the correct behavior. Providing opportunities for role playing or practice of correct behaviors provides for a higher frequency of these behaviors. Yet there is one further component of Structured Learning to consider, a component responsive to the ultimate purpose of any teaching endeavor: transfer of what has been learned from the Structured Learning teaching setting to the classroom or other real-life settings.

TRANSFER OF TRAINING

The main interest of any teaching program, and where most teaching programs fail, is not in students' performance during the training activity, but, instead, in how well they perform in their real lives. If skills have been satisfactorily performed at the time of teaching, what procedures are available to maximize the chances that such performance will consistently continue on the street, in school, at home, or in other places or situations where skill use is appropriate? In other words, how can transfer of training be encouraged?

ENHANCERS OF TRANSFER OF TRAINING

Research has identified a number of principles of transfer enhancement. Attending to all these principles greatly increases the likelihood of successful transfer. These principles will be described in the rest of this chapter, and their incorporation into Structured Learning will be examined in subsequent chapters. Transfer and maintenance of learned behaviors may be enhanced by (1) the teaching setting, materials, and personnel, (2) reinforcement systems, and (3) task instruction.

Teaching Setting, Materials, and Personnel

Generalization or transfer is facilitated when the setting in which the teaching occurs closely resembles the natural setting where the skill will be used. It has been demonstrated repeatedly that the greater the number of *identical elements* or characteristics shared by the teaching and application settings, the greater the later transfer from teaching to real-life application. Ideally, both the interpersonal and physical characteristics of the teaching and application settings would be similar in as many ways as possible. Thus, if possible, the students would be instructed along with other children with whom they interact regularly. Also, the teaching would take place to the extent feasible in school settings or in other real-life environments in which the students actually interact, rather than at a therapy or instructional center or psychologist/counselor's office. When this is not possible, and simulation must be used in lieu of teaching in the natural environment, the physical setting (i.e., furnishings, materials) should be as much like the natural setting as possible (Buckley & Walker, 1978). Using props and arranging the teaching environment to resemble the real-life environment where the skill should be performed will likely enhance transfer.

The actual use of a skill is facilitated by teaching the skill in a *variety of settings and in response to a variety of persons* (Stokes & Baer, 1977; Stokes, Baer, & Jackson, 1974). Several researchers have demonstrated that transfer is greater when a variety of such teaching stimuli are employed (Callantine & Warren, 1955; Duncan, 1958; Shore & Sechrest, 1961). The use of several different school settings, models, teachers, and role-playing co-actors in Structured Learning is based on this principle of transfer enhancement.

An additional method of facilitating transfer focuses on changes in the environment that will support the child's new behavior (Walker, 1979). The needs of the students are all too likely to be forgotten once they "graduate" and leave the teaching environment for real-life settings. The efforts until "graduation day" may have been educationally perfect and the students may have performed the skills at a high level of excellence. Yet, given these successful efforts, the teaching may fail if it is discontinued at this point. Teaching provides skills, information, knowledge, and the potential for successful application. However, it is primarily *real-life reinforcement*—by teachers, parents, peers, and the students themselves—that will determine if the learning will endure. Homework assignments are a major vehicle for presenting opportunities for real-life experience and reinforcement. The nature and format of such assignments will be discussed in Chapter 5.

Reinforcement Systems

The importance of continued, intermittent reinforcement for lasting behavior change should be stressed. Are the new behaviors ignored? Or, as is perhaps more common, are they reinforced at first and then ignored? Continued reinforcement, though gradually thinned or more intermittent, is clearly a necessary part of enduring transfer of training. When implementing a Structured Learning program for skill-deficient children, it is highly desirable for the teacher to attempt to train parents, principals, other teachers, other school personnel, and peers how to provide students with continued real-life reinforcement. Such reinforcement must take into account all the dimensions of reinforcement (scheduling, nature, amount, etc.) discussed earlier as crucial aspects of the performance feedback process. Using reinforcements during Structured Learning that may also occur naturally in the environment, such as smiling and a pleasant thank you, will increase the chances that the student will be responsive to reinforcement by others outside of the teaching setting (Stokes & Baer, 1977).

Task Instruction

It has been well established that practiced behavior, or behavior that has occurred frequently in the past, will be more likely to occur in future situations. This principle originates from research on overlearning, which demonstrates that the higher the degree of original learning, the greater the probability of later transfer. In the context of Structured Learning, this means that the greater the number of correct enactments of a given skill during role playing, the more likely it is that the skill will transfer. In addition to increasing the likelihood of positive transfer, overlearning may also decrease the chances that negative transfer (interference rather than facilitation) will occur. When more than one skill is being taught, negative transfer or interference with learning is likely to occur if instruction on the second skill is begun while the first is still only partially learned. This is less likely to occur when correct skill behavior is practiced enough to insure that overlearning has occurred.

Even though a student has learned a skill well in the Structured Learning setting, it is desirable for transfer-enhancement purposes that the instruction be withdrawn systematically, rather than stopped abruptly (Buckley & Walker, 1978). Periodic review of the learned skills (booster sessions) will assist with such systematic fading of instruction.

Describing to students the specific types of situations in the real world in which they should use a given skill is called Instructed Generalization (Stokes & Baer, 1977). Students can be encouraged to use a particular skill in a variety of natural problematic situations and real-life settings. Historically, teachers have used this principle of generalization by instructing students in what to do at the "teachable moment" or when the skill is actually needed. Thus, giving reminders or instructions to the students when the need arises is an easily implemented and valuable principle to enhance transfer.

Table 1 summarizes all of the transfer and maintenance strategies that ideally should be incorporated into Structured Learning instruction.

SUMMARY

Four procedures for teaching prosocial skills—modeling, role playing, performance feedback, and transfer of training—have been examined. The nature of each, the techniques that maximize their effectiveness, and samples of supporting research

Table 1. Transfer and Maintenance Strategies

TEACHING SETTING, MATERIALS, AND PERSONNEL

1. Instruction in natural environments where the skill is actually needed (e.g., playground, hallways, school bus) (Walker, 1979).
2. Teaching in a setting that is similar to those environments where the skill is to be used (Goldstein, 1981).
3. Using props to enhance the similarity of the teaching setting and the natural setting (Buckley & Walker, 1978).
4. Teaching peers, teachers, parents, and others to reinforce skill use (Stokes, Baer, & Jackson, 1974).
5. Teaching the skill in the context of a variety of situations and settings by multiple role plays with different persons (Stokes & Baer, 1977; Wahler, 1969).

REINFORCEMENT SYSTEMS

6. Providing reinforcement immediately following the desired behavior (Stokes & Baer, 1977).
7. Providing reinforcement on an intermittent schedule (Stokes & Baer, 1977).
8. Gradually decreasing the frequency of reinforcement for desired performance (Koegel & Rincover, 1977).
9. Providing for natural reinforcement, that is, reinforcement that is likely to occur in the natural environment, paired with other reinforcement as needed (Stokes & Baer, 1977).

TASK INSTRUCTION

10. Overlearning the skill by practice several times in different sets of circumstances, multiple role plays, homework assignments (Goldstein, 1981).
11. Systematic withdrawal of instruction by periodic review and reteaching of the skills as needed (Buckley & Walker, 1978).
12. Instructing the student to use the skill when conditions indicate the skill could be used (Stokes & Baer, 1977).
13. Planning for opportunities where students can practice the prosocial skills they learned in the teaching session (Cartledge & Milburn, 1980).

have been presented. Yet, in discussing each procedure, we raised one or more notes of caution. For example, while modeling does result in the learning of new behaviors, without sufficient practice old behaviors tend to recur. Practice or role playing is also an important aid to new learning, but the behaviors practiced must be correct, which may be more likely when illustrated by prior modeling. Given both modeling and role playing, the newly learned behaviors are more likely to persist. Yet this will not occur unless the student sees her use of these behaviors as a rewarding experience: thus, the necessity for reinforcement. Also, the behaviors must be performed by the student correctly and with sufficient frequency that the opportunity for reinforcement occurs often enough. Without this, the new behaviors, even if reinforced, may occur too seldom for stable learning to take place. Procedures such as modeling and role playing can lead to sufficient frequency of correct performance. Combining these three procedures provides a much more effective approach to skill instruction. Yet, a truly effective approach must also demonstrate learning beyond the teaching setting. Thus, we turned in our discussion to transfer of training and presented several principles that enhance the likelihood that skills learned in the teaching environment will transfer to the student's real-life setting.

CHAPTER 3

Assessment for Selection and Grouping

This chapter will describe techniques for selecting and grouping students in order to enhance their skill acquisition through Structured Learning. Using the methods presented, the teacher will be able to identify children's skill strengths and weaknesses, assign them to specific groups for instruction, and evaluate each child's progress through Structured Learning. The goal is to arrive at a teaching prescription tailored to the individual skill assets and deficits of each child.

IDENTIFICATION OF POTENTIAL PARTICIPANTS IN STRUCTURED LEARNING

Interviews, self-reports, naturalistic observation, analogue observation, behavior rating scales, and sociometrics are among the behavioral techniques available to educators for identifying students who are weak or lacking in prosocial behaviors.

INTERVIEWS

Interviews conducted to obtain skill-relevant information for selection and grouping purposes may be conducted with the children themselves as well as with parents, teachers, or others.

Student Interviews

Many children are aware of their own ability or lack of ability to deal with others in constructive or positive ways. Furthermore, they can often identify the specific areas in the social sphere in which they would like to become more competent. Cartledge and Milburn (1980) suggest several social skill-relevant areas that could be explored in a student interview format:

1. The ability to express opinions contrary to those of peers, parents, and teachers;
2. The ability to ask favors of someone;
3. The ability to initiate conversations with peers and adults;
4. The ability to refuse unreasonable requests from friends and strangers;
5. The ability to invite a peer to play;
6. The ability to compliment someone;
7. The ability to receive compliments;
8. The ability to ask for help in solving problems;
9. The ability to resist pressure from peers to behave in an unacceptable way. (p. 45)

Although the student interview method can provide much-needed information regarding a child's self-perceptions, some students may be reluctant to engage in such an interview, and therefore an accurate initial picture of the child may not be ascertained if an interview alone is relied upon. However, the student interview may be viewed as a useful way to begin identifying particular students who may benefit from Structured Learning and to gather information regarding the specific skills the students view as most useful for them to learn.

Interviews with Others in the Child's Environment

Information gathered, when it is appropriate to do so, from interviews with a child's parents and teachers, is valuable in selecting students for social skills intervention. Ask questions such as: Does the child comply with requests? If not, how does the child respond? Does the child have friends in the neighborhood and at school? In what ways does the child deal with interpersonal relationships and feelings such as anger and frustration? The answers to such questions can indicate to the teacher which children are perceived by others as experiencing difficulty with social behaviors in and out of the classroom.

SELF-REPORTS

Inventories completed by the students can provide information relevant to selection for Structured Learning, although the way students respond to such inventories must always be evaluated in terms of possible defensiveness or "answering the way they feel they *should*." This information can also be used to reveal discrepancies between teacher and student perceptions, to identify critical skills for teaching, and to assess changes in the student's self-statements (pre- and postinstruction).

The Student Skill Checklist, described and presented later in this chapter, is the self-report measure we have developed and found quite useful for selection, grouping, and evaluation purposes. Two other recently developed self-report measures that may be particularly valuable for these purposes are the Children's Action Tendency Scale (Deluty, 1979) and the Children's Assertive Behavior Scale (Wood, Michelson, & Flynn, Note 2). The first measures aggressiveness, assertiveness, and submissiveness; the second is an assertiveness measure. For very young children and those with reading difficulties, these measures—as well as the Student Skill Checklist—will more appropriately be used as question lists or schedules for a structured interview, rather than as self-report inventories.

NATURALISTIC OBSERVATION

Direct observation in classroom or other contexts may also advantageously be used to assess a child's skill-relevant behavior. In this process, the teacher or other observer watches what the child does at particular times or in particular situations. This information is most often coded and reported in relevant categories of behavior (e.g., amount of time spent interacting with peers, number of questions asked in class). A variety of observation and recording techniques exist. Frequency counts (listing the number of occurrences of behaviors in specific social areas such as negative peer interaction, joining in games appropriately, staying out of fights), duration recording (recording the length of time a student engages in either an appropriate or inappropriate social behavior), and anecdotal records (a daily listing of a child's specific problematic behaviors and when they occur) are examples of observation methods that can easily be implemented by classroom teachers. Other, more complicated observational systems yield information not only about a particular student's behavior, but also about the behavior of his peers in the same setting (Fitzgerald, 1979; Hops, Fleischman, Guild, Paine, Street, Walker, & Greenwood, 1978; Greenwood, Walker, Todd, & Hops, Note 3).

Although these direct observational methods have the advantage of being concrete and specific, students may be aware of being observed and behave differently than when they are not observed. Therefore, several observations may be needed to assess the student's typical behavior. Asking the classroom teacher to indicate whether the observed behaviors appear to be typical for the student also may assist in offsetting this problem. A further difficulty with observational methods is that the behaviors observed in one situation may not necessarily be representative of what the student would do in other situations. Thus, observations across a variety of school settings will be necessary in order to obtain the most accurate information about the child's social interaction.

ANALOGUE OBSERVATION

Because naturalistic observation is time consuming and sufficient personnel are often not available to observe the students' behaviors adequately, an alternative method is to conduct simulation activities in which certain aspects of the natural environment are staged and the student's behavior in that situation is then observed. For instance, instead of attempting to observe actual interactions between students and "authority figures," one could construct a simulation in the form of a role-playing task in which a student must interact with the school's principal. This interaction can be more readily observed and recorded in a standardized manner than a similar real-life interaction. However, it must be recognized that such simulations lose the spontaneity of real-life encounters and thus may elicit more atypical behaviors.

Analogue observation may be useful not only for selection purposes, but for grouping students as well. This can be done by the creation of "trial groups," such as those described by Goldstein, Heller, and Sechrest (1966). These authors suggest that one of the best predictors of how a person will behave in a group situation is to observe that person in a similar type of group setting. In Structured Learning this might be done by placing students in a trial Structured Learning group for two or three sessions to observe how they perform. Are they able to maintain attention for at least 15 minutes? Can they under-stand what is going on? Do they follow teacher instructions? Can they role play? If the children can meet these minimal criteria in the trial group, their success in doing so in more permanent Structured Learning groups is likely.

BEHAVIOR RATING SCALES

Another beneficial approach to identification of skill-deficient children is the use of behavior rating scales (Greenwood, Walker, & Hops, 1977). In this method the observer (e.g., a teacher who has had ongoing opportunities to observe the student) is presented with a list of relevant behaviors to rate according to their intensity (how much), their frequency (how often), or other criteria. A variety of individuals—teachers, par-ents, other school personnel—may react to the child's behavior using this method. Thus, useful information can be gathered from several sources without necessarily involving the child. Examples of some behavior rating scales designed for use with elementary school children include the Quay-Peterson Behavior Problem Checklist (Quay & Peterson, 1967), the Walker Problem Behavior Identification Checklist (Walker, 1970), and the Hahnemann Elementary School Behavior Rating Scale (Spivak & Swift, 1975).

Social skills inventories are behavior rating scales in which the items to be rated are skill behaviors. The Student Skill Checklist provided later in this chapter is one such measure. A second selection and grouping instrument, in this instance to be completed by the teacher or someone else very familiar with the child's behavior, is the Teacher Skill Checklist. We have found this measure to be an especially valuable tool for selection and grouping purposes. It, too, appears in full later in this chapter.

SOCIOMETRICS

Children who demonstrate inappropriate social behaviors may also lack acceptance by their peers (Barclay, 1966). Patterson, Reid, Jones, & Conger (1975) and Rathjen (1980) suggest that friendliness, social participation, and outgoing behavior are characteristic of children who perceive themselves as accepted by peers, while aggressive behavior is often associated with peer rejection. Although sociometrics have been criticized as intrusive (O'Leary & Johnson, 1979), the information gained from such peer ratings is frequently important for selection and grouping purposes.

For classroom teachers, peer nominations, peer ratings, and other sociometric information can point out particular students who are experiencing difficulties in positively interacting with other children. This information may confirm a teacher's tentative observations. Sociometric information may also help to identify a student who is shy or somewhat withdrawn and who thus may be easily overlooked as a child to be targeted for Structured Learning instruction. Such children may not be accepted by their peer group, and their need to learn prosocial behaviors may be as great, if not greater, than that of the aggressive child.

The peer nomination method consists of instructing students to list a number of classmates according to specific criteria (e.g., who they would like most to play with, work with, or sit next to, or who they are best friends with). Students may also be told to list the classmates they would least like to be associated with in order to assess which students appear to lack friendship-making skills. The peer rating (or roster rating) method involves peer rating of every student in the class according to predetermined criteria. Such methods facilitate the identification of children who are neither chosen as friends nor rejected, but tend toward social isolation. These children may also benefit from the Structure Learning approach.

Each of the selection and grouping techniques just described has its own strengths and weaknesses. A comprehensive picture of a particular child's social competence can be gained by implementing appropriate combinations of these methods, thus more fully identifying children who are in need of social skills intervention than by using any one method alone.

STUDENT SKILL CHECKLIST

Teachers may request that students complete the Student Skill Checklist (Figure 1), which is designed to assess students' perceptions of the skills they feel they need to learn. This self-rating may contribute to students' awareness of the skills that might be taught to them through Structured Learning. It may also increase their willingness to participate in Structured Learning activities if completing the Checklist sensitizes them to the relevance of the skills to their effectiveness and thereby to more satisfactory peer interactions. The Student Skill Checklist is written at a third-grade reading level and is suggested for students at this level. This checklist may be simplified by the teacher and read to younger students individually or in small group settings. Due to the length of the Checklist, the teacher may wish to give only a part of it at one time. Depending upon the length of time the students are able to attend to this task, it may take more than one or two sessions to complete the entire Checklist.

TEACHER SKILL CHECKLIST

The Teacher Skill Checklist (Figure 2) is completed by a teacher or other person who is familiar with the student's behaviors in a variety of situations. This Checklist requires the rater to respond to descriptions of the skills taught in Structured Learning in terms of the frequency of a particular student's use of the skill. It also provides an opportunity for the rater to identify situations in which skill use is particularly problematic. Thus the student's skill behaviors can be rated and summarized, yielding a numerical proficiency value for each skill and pinpointing the particular situations associated with difficulty in skill use.

SKILL TRAINING GROUPING CHART

Information from the Teacher and Student Skill Checklists may be used to group students on the basis of shared skill deficiencies. The student's name and ratings on each skill are entered on the Skill Training Grouping Chart (Figure 3), thus providing a visual summary of ratings of individual strengths and weaknesses in all skills. By listing both the teacher's rating and the student's rating on each skill, the teacher can also easily note

Figure 1. Student Skill Checklist

Name: _____   Date: _____

Directions: Each of the questions will ask you about how well you do something. Next to each question is a number.

  Circle number 1 if you *almost never* do what the question asks.
  Circle number 2 if you *seldom* do it.
  Circle number 3 if you *sometimes* do it.
  Circle number 4 if you do it *often.*
  Circle number 5 if you *almost always* do it.

There are no right or wrong answers to these questions. Answer the way you really feel about each question.

Ratings:

1	2	3	4	5
Almost Never	Seldom	Sometimes	Often	Almost Always

	Almost Never	Seldom	Sometimes	Often	Almost Always
1. Is it easy for me to listen to someone who is talking to me?	1	2	3	4	5
2. Do I ask for help in a friendly way when I need the help?	1	2	3	4	5
3. Do I tell people thank you for something they have done for me?	1	2	3	4	5
4. Do I have the materials I need for my classes (like books, pencils, paper)?	1	2	3	4	5
5. Do I understand what to do when directions are given and do I follow these directions?	1	2	3	4	5
6. Do I finish my schoolwork?	1	2	3	4	5
7. Do I join in on class talks or discussions?	1	2	3	4	5
8. Do I try to help an adult when I think he/she could use the help?	1	2	3	4	5
9. Do I decide what I don't understand about my schoolwork and ask my teacher the question in a friendly way?	1	2	3	4	5
10. Is it easy for me to keep doing my schoolwork when people are noisy?	1	2	3	4	5
11. Do I fix mistakes on my work without getting upset?	1	2	3	4	5
12. Do I choose something to do when I have free time?	1	2	3	4	5
13. Do I decide on something I want to work for and keep working until I get it?	1	2	3	4	5

	Almost Never	Seldom	Sometimes	Often	Almost Always
14. Is it easy for me to take the first step to meet somebody I don't know?	1	2	3	4	5
15. Is it easy for me to start a conversation with someone?	1	2	3	4	5
16. When I have something else I have to do, do I end a conversation with someone in a nice way?	1	2	3	4	5
17. Do I ask to join in a game or activity in a friendly way?	1	2	3	4	5
18. Do I follow the rules when I play a game?	1	2	3	4	5
19. Is it easy for me to ask a favor of someone?	1	2	3	4	5
20. Do I notice when somebody needs help and try to help them?	1	2	3	4	5
21. Do I tell others that I like something nice about them or something nice they have done for me or for somebody else?	1	2	3	4	5
22. When someone says they like something about me, do I accept what they say?	1	2	3	4	5
23. Do I suggest things to do with my friends?	1	2	3	4	5
24. Am I willing to share my things with others?	1	2	3	4	5
25. Do I tell others I'm sorry after I do something wrong?	1	2	3	4	5
26. Do I know how I feel about different things that happen?	1	2	3	4	5
27. Do I let others know what I am feeling and do it in a good way?	1	2	3	4	5
28. Do I try to tell how other people are feeling?	1	2	3	4	5
29. Do I show others that I understand how they feel?	1	2	3	4	5
30. When someone has a problem, do I let them know that I understand how they feel?	1	2	3	4	5
31. When I am angry, do I deal with it in ways that won't hurt other people?	1	2	3	4	5
32. Do I try to understand other people's angry feelings?	1	2	3	4	5
33. Do I let others know I care about them?	1	2	3	4	5
34. Do I know what makes me afraid and do I think of things to do so I don't stay afraid?	1	2	3	4	5
35. Do I say and do nice things for myself when I have earned it?	1	2	3	4	5
36. Do I keep my temper when I am upset?	1	2	3	4	5
37. Do I know when I have to ask to do something I want to do, and do I ask in a friendly way?	1	2	3	4	5
38. When somebody teases me, do I stay in control?	1	2	3	4	5
39. Do I try to stay away from things that may get me into trouble?	1	2	3	4	5

Figure 1. *(continued)*

	Almost Never	Seldom	Sometimes	Often	Almost Always
40. Do I think of ways other than fighting to take care of problems?	1	2	3	4	5
41. Do I think of ways to deal with a problem and think of what might happen if I use these ways?	1	2	3	4	5
42. When I do something I shouldn't have done, do I accept what happens then?	1	2	3	4	5
43. Do I decide what I have been accused of and why, and then think of a good way to handle it?	1	2	3	4	5
44. When I don't agree with somebody, do I help think of a plan to make both of us happy?	1	2	3	4	5
45. When I feel bored, do I think of good things to do and then do them?	1	2	3	4	5
46. Do I know when a problem happened because of something I did?	1	2	3	4	5
47. Do I tell others without getting mad or yelling when they have caused a problem for me?	1	2	3	4	5
48. Do I help think of a fair way to take care of a complaint against me?	1	2	3	4	5
49. When I lose at a game do I keep from getting upset?	1	2	3	4	5
50. Do I tell others something good about the way they played a game?	1	2	3	4	5
51. Do I decide if I have been left out, and then do things in a good way to make me feel better?	1	2	3	4	5
52. Do I do things that will help me feel less embarrassed?	1	2	3	4	5
53. When I don't do well with something (on a test, doing my chores), do I decide ways I could do better next time?	1	2	3	4	5
54. When I am told no, can I keep from becoming upset?	1	2	3	4	5
55. Do I say no to things that might get me into trouble or that I don't want to do, and do I say it in a friendly way?	1	2	3	4	5
56. Can I keep my body from getting tight and tense when I'm angry or upset?	1	2	3	4	5
57. When a group of kids wants me to do something that might get me in trouble or that is wrong, do I say no?	1	2	3	4	5
58. Do I keep from taking things that aren't mine?	1	2	3	4	5
59. Is it easy for me to decide what to do when I'm given a choice?	1	2	3	4	5
60. Do I tell the truth about what I have done, even if I might get into trouble?	1	2	3	4	5

Figure 2. Teacher Skill Checklist

Student: _____   Class: _____

Date: _____   Teacher: _____

Directions: Listed below you will find a number of skills that children are more or less proficient in using. This checklist will help you record how well each child uses the various skills. For each child, rate his/her use of each skill, based on your observations of his/her behavior in various situations.

Circle 1 if the child is *almost never* good at using the skill.
Circle 2 if the child is *seldom* good at using the skill.
Circle 3 if the child is *sometimes* good at using the skill.
Circle 4 if the child is *often* good at using the skill.
Circle 5 if the child is *almost always* good at using the skill.

Please rate the child on all skills listed. If you know of a situation in which the child has particular difficulty in using the skill well, please note it briefly in the space marked "Problem Situation."

	Almost Never	Seldom	Sometimes	Often	Almost Always

1. **Listening:** Does the student appear to listen when someone is speaking and make an effort to understand what is said?   1 2 3 4 5

Problem Situation: _____

2. **Asking for Help:** Does the student decide when he/she needs assistance and ask for this help in a pleasant manner?   1 2 3 4 5

Problem Situation: _____

3. **Saying Thank You:** Does the student tell others he/she appreciates help given, favors, etc.?   1 2 3 4 5

Problem Situation: _____

4. **Bringing Materials to Class:** Does the student remember the books and materials he/she needs for class?   1 2 3 4 5

Problem Situation: _____

5. **Following Instructions:** Does the student understand instructions and follow them?   1 2 3 4 5

Problem Situation: _____

Figure 2. *(continued)*

	Almost Never	Seldom	Sometimes	Often	Almost Always
6. **Completing Assignments:** Does the student complete assignments at his/her independent academic level?	1	2	3	4	5

Problem Situation: _____

7. **Contributing to Discussions:** Does the student participate in class discussions in accordance with the classroom rules?   1 2 3 4 5

Problem Situation: _____

8. **Offering Help to an Adult:** Does the student offer to help you at appropriate times and in an appropriate manner?   1 2 3 4 5

Problem Situation: _____

9. **Asking a Question:** Does the student know how and when to ask a question of another person?   1 2 3 4 5

Problem Situation: _____

10. **Ignoring Distractions:** Does the student ignore classroom distractions?   1 2 3 4 5

Problem Situation: _____

11. **Making Corrections:** Does the student make the necessary corrections on assignments without getting overly frustrated?   1 2 3 4 5

Problem Situation: _____

12. **Deciding on Something to Do:** Does the student find something to do when he/she has free time?   1 2 3 4 5

Problem Situation: _____

13. **Setting a Goal:** Does the student set realistic goals for himself/herself and take the necessary steps to meet these goals?   1 2 3 4 5

Problem Situation: _____

	Almost Never	Seldom	Sometimes	Often	Almost Always

14. **Introducing Yourself:** Does the student introduce himself/herself to people he/she doesn't know in an appropriate way?   1 2 3 4 5

Problem Situation: _____

15. **Beginning a Conversation:** Does the student know how and when to begin a conversation with another person?   1 2 3 4 5

Problem Situation: _____

16. **Ending a Conversation:** Does the student end a conversation when it's necessary and in an appropriate manner?   1 2 3 4 5

Problem Situation: _____

17. **Joining In:** Does the student know and practice acceptable ways of joining an ongoing activity or group?   1 2 3 4 5

Problem Situation: _____

18. **Playing a Game:** Does the student play games with classmates fairly?   1 2 3 4 5

Problem Situation: _____

19. **Asking a Favor:** Does the student know how to ask a favor of another person in a pleasant manner?   1 2 3 4 5

Problem Situation: _____

20. **Offering Help to a Classmate:** Can the student recognize when someone needs or wants assistance and offer this help?   1 2 3 4 5

Problem Situation: _____

21. **Giving a Compliment:** Does the student tell others that he/she likes something about them or something they have done?   1 2 3 4 5

Problem Situation: _____

Figure 2. *(continued)*

	Almost Never	Seldom	Sometimes	Often	Almost Always

22. **Accepting a Compliment:** Does the student accept these comments given by adults or his/her peers in a friendly way?   1 2 3 4 5

Problem Situation: _____

23. **Suggesting an Activity:** Does the student suggest appropriate activities to others?   1 2 3 4 5

Problem Situation: _____

24. **Sharing:** Is the student agreeable to sharing things with others, and if not, does he/she offer reasons why he/she can't in an acceptable manner?   1 2 3 4 5

Problem Situation: _____

25. **Apologizing:** Does the student tell others he/she is sorry for doing something in a sincere manner?   1 2 3 4 5

Problem Situation: _____

26. **Knowing Your Feelings:** Does the student identify feelings he/she is experiencing?   1 2 3 4 5

Problem Situation: _____

27. **Expressing Your Feelings:** Does the student express his/her feelings in acceptable ways?   1 2 3 4 5

Problem Situation: _____

28. **Recognizing Another's Feelings:** Does the student try to figure out how others are feeling in acceptable ways?   1 2 3 4 5

Problem Situation: _____

29. **Showing Understanding of Another's Feelings:** Does the student show understanding of others' feelings in acceptable ways?   1 2 3 4 5

Problem Situation: _____

	Almost Never	Seldom	Sometimes	Often	Almost Always

30. **Expressing Concern for Another:** Does the student express concern for others in acceptable ways? 1 2 3 4 5

Problem Situation: _____

31. **Dealing with Your Anger:** Does the student use acceptable ways to express his/her anger? 1 2 3 4 5

Problem Situation: _____

32. **Dealing with Another's Anger:** Does the student try to understand another's anger without getting angry himself/herself? 1 2 3 4 5

Problem Situation: _____

33. **Expressing Affection:** Does the student let others know he/she cares about them in an acceptable manner? 1 2 3 4 5

Problem Situation: _____

34. **Dealing with Fear:** Does the student know why he/she is afraid and practice strategies to reduce this fear? 1 2 3 4 5

Problem Situation: _____

35. **Rewarding Yourself:** Does the student say and do nice things for himself/herself when a reward is deserved? 1 2 3 4 5

Problem Situation: _____

36. **Using Self-control:** Does the student know and practice strategies to control his/her temper or excitement? 1 2 3 4 5

Problem Situation: _____

37. **Asking Permission:** Does the student know when and how to ask if he/she may do something? 1 2 3 4 5

Problem Situation: _____

38. **Responding to Teasing:** Does the student deal with being teased in ways that allow him/her to remain in control? 1 2 3 4 5

Problem Situation: _____

Figure 2. *(continued)*

	Almost Never	Seldom	Sometimes	Often	Almost Always

39. **Avoiding Trouble:** Does the student stay away from situations that may get him/her into trouble?   1   2   3   4   5

Problem Situation: _____

40. **Staying Out of Fights:** Does the student know of and practice socially appropriate ways of handling potential fights?   1   2   3   4   5

Problem Situation: _____

41. **Problem Solving:** When a problem occurs, does the student think of alternatives and choose an alternative, then evaluate how well this solved the problem?   1   2   3   4   5

Problem Situation: _____

42. **Accepting Consequences:** Does the student accept the consequences for his/her behavior without becoming defensive or upset?   1   2   3   4   5

Problem Situation: _____

43. **Dealing with an Accusation:** Does the student know of and practice ways to deal with being accused of something?   1   2   3   4   5

Problem Situation: _____

44. **Negotiating:** Is the student willing to give and take in order to reach a compromise?   1   2   3   4   5

Problem Situation: _____

45. **Dealing with Boredom:** Does the student select acceptable activities when he/she is bored?   1   2   3   4   5

Problem Situation: _____

46. **Deciding What Caused a Problem:** Does the student assess what caused a problem and accept the responsibility if appropriate?   1   2   3   4   5

Problem Situation: _____

47. **Making a Complaint:** Does the student know how to say that he/she disagrees in acceptable ways? 1 2 3 4 5

Problem Situation: _____

48. **Answering a Complaint:** Is the student willing to arrive at a fair solution to someone's justified complaint? 1 2 3 4 5

Problem Situation: _____

49. **Dealing with Losing:** Does the student accept losing at a game or activity without becoming upset or angry? 1 2 3 4 5

Problem Situation: _____

50. **Showing Sportsmanship:** Does the student express a sincere compliment to others about how they played the game? 1 2 3 4 5

Problem Situation: _____

51. **Dealing with Being Left Out:** Does the student deal with being left out of an activity without losing control? 1 2 3 4 5

Problem Situation: _____

52. **Dealing with Embarrassment:** Does the student know of things to do that help him/her feel less embarrassed or self-conscious? 1 2 3 4 5

Problem Situation: _____

53. **Reacting to Failure:** Does the student figure out the reason(s) for his/her failure, and how he/she can be more successful the next time? 1 2 3 4 5

Problem Situation: _____

54. **Accepting No:** Does the student accept being told no without becoming unduly upset or angry? 1 2 3 4 5

Problem Situation: _____

Figure 2. *(continued)*

	Almost Never	Seldom	Sometimes	Often	Almost Always

55. **Saying No:** Does the student say no in acceptable ways to things he/she doesn't want to do or to things that may get him/her into trouble?   1 2 3 4 5

Problem Situation: _____

56. **Relaxing:** Is the student able to relax when tense or upset?   1 2 3 4 5

Problem Situation: _____

57. **Dealing with Group Pressure:** Does the student decide what he/she wants to do when others pressure him/her to do something else?   1 2 3 4 5

Problem Situation: _____

58. **Dealing with Wanting Something That Isn't Mine:** Does the student refrain from taking things that don't belong to him/her?   1 2 3 4 5

Problem Situation: _____

59. **Making a Decision:** Does the student make thoughtful choices?   1 2 3 4 5

Problem Situation: _____

60. **Being Honest:** Is the student honest when confronted with a negative action?   1 2 3 4 5

Problem Situation: _____

Figure 3. Grouping Chart

	Student Names											
I. Classroom Survival Skills												
1. Listening												
2. Asking for Help												
3. Saying Thank You												
4. Bringing Materials to Class												
5. Following Instructions												
6. Completing Assignments												
7. Contributing to Discussions												
8. Offering Help to an Adult												
9. Asking a Question												
10. Ignoring Distractions												
11. Making Corrections												
12. Deciding on Something to Do												
13. Setting a Goal												
II. Friendship-Making Skills												
14. Introducing Yourself												
15. Beginning a Conversation												
16. Ending a Conversation												
17. Joining In												
18. Playing a Game												
19. Asking a Favor												
20. Offering Help to a Classmate												
21. Giving a Compliment												
22. Accepting a Compliment												
23. Suggesting an Activity												
24. Sharing												
25. Apologizing												
III. Skills for Dealing with Feelings												
26. Knowing Your Feelings												
27. Expressing Your Feelings												
28. Recognizing Another's Feelings												
29. Showing Understanding of Another's Feelings												
30. Expressing Concern for Another												

Figure 3. *(continued)*

	Student Names												
III. Skills for Dealing with Feelings (cont.)													
31. Dealing with Your Anger													
32. Dealing with Another's Anger													
33. Expressing Affection													
34. Dealing with Fear													
35. Rewarding Yourself													
IV. Skill Alternatives to Aggression													
36. Using Self-control													
37. Asking Permission													
38. Responding to Teasing													
39. Avoiding Trouble													
40. Staying Out of Fights													
41. Problem Solving													
42. Accepting Consequences													
43. Dealing with an Accusation													
44. Negotiating													
V. Skills for Dealing with Stress													
45. Dealing with Boredom													
46. Deciding What Caused a Problem													
47. Making a Complaint													
48. Answering a Complaint													
49. Dealing with Losing													
50. Showing Sportsmanship													
51. Dealing with Being Left Out													
52. Dealing with Embarrassment													
53. Reacting to Failure													
54. Accepting No													
55. Saying No													
56. Relaxing													
57. Dealing with Group Pressure													
58. Dealing with Wanting Something That Isn't Mine													
59. Making a Decision													
60. Being Honest													

where discrepancies between the ratings exist. The teacher can then evaluate these differences in terms of unrealistic or overly critical self-perceptions on the part of the student, possible student defensiveness, and overly high or low teacher expectations for the student's behavior. The teacher should scan the charts for low ratings (*1*s or *2*s on *either* the Teacher or the Student Skill Checklist) within the same skill group and then, if possible, assign youngsters with similar patterns to particular Structured Learning groups.

In instances where the entire class will be instructed in Structured Learning as one unit, as in a small special education classroom, for example, a greater range of skill proficiencies and deficiencies will likely be apparent. In this case, entering the teacher and student ratings for each student onto the Grouping Chart will provide a profile of the class as a whole. The teacher then has the option of selecting as starting skills those that many class members show a deficiency in.

PROGRESS SUMMARY SHEET

The teacher may use the Progress Summary Sheet (Figure 4) to record each student's skill level from the Teacher Skill Checklist and the Student Skill Checklist before and after participation in Structured Learning. This method provides a record of the consistency or specific discrepancies between the teacher's and the student's ratings and also assists in discerning increased proficiency in each skill for which Structured Learning was undertaken.

STUDENT MASTERY RECORD

The Student Mastery Record (Figure 5) is useful in three important ways. First, if used publicly, having students record their own mastery of a skill creates an open acknowledgment of achievement, which often heightens motivation for further skill acquisition and transfer. Second, it defines the behavioral objectives or goals relevant to particular students. Teachers, counselors, school psychologists, and others are required in many cases, such as when working with special education students, to define what is to be accomplished for each student

Figure 4. Progress Summary Sheet

Student: _____

Date: _____

	Teacher Pretest Score Date: ___	Student Pretest Score Date: ___	Teacher Posttest Score Date: ___	Student Posttest Score Date: ___	Performance Change Pretest –Posttest Teacher	Student
I. Classroom Survival Skills						
1. Listening						
2. Asking for Help						
3. Saying Thank You						
4. Bringing Materials to Class						
5. Following Instructions						
6. Completing Assignments						
7. Contributing to Discussions						
8. Offering Help to an Adult						
9. Asking a Question						
10. Ignoring Distractions						
11. Making Corrections						
12. Deciding on Something to Do						
13. Setting a Goal						
II. Friendship-Making Skills						
14. Introducing Yourself						
15. Beginning a Conversation						
16. Ending a Conversation						
17. Joining In						
18. Playing a Game						
19. Asking a Favor						
20. Offering Help to a Classmate						

	Teacher Pretest Score Date: ___	Student Pretest Score Date: ___	Teacher Posttest Score Date: ___	Student Posttest Score Date: ___	Performance Change Pretest –Posttest Teacher	Student
II. Friendship-Making Skills (cont.)						
21. Giving a Compliment						
22. Accepting a Compliment						
23. Suggesting an Activity						
24. Sharing						
25. Apologizing						
III. Skills for Dealing with Feelings						
26. Knowing Your Feelings						
27. Expressing Your Feelings						
28. Recognizing Another's Feelings						
29. Showing Understanding of Another's Feelings						
30. Expressing Concern for Another						
31. Dealing with Your Anger						
32. Dealing with Another's Anger						
33. Expressing Affection						
34. Dealing with Fear						
35. Rewarding Yourself						
IV. Skill Alternatives to Aggression						
36. Using Self-control						
37. Asking Permission						
38. Responding to Teasing						
39. Avoiding Trouble						
40. Staying Out of Fights						

Figure 4. *(continued)*

	Teacher Pretest Score Date: ___	Student Pretest Score Date: ___	Teacher Posttest Score Date: ___	Student Posttest Score Date: ___	Performance Change Pretest–Posttest Teacher	Student
IV. Skill Alternatives to Aggression (cont.)						
41. Problem Solving						
42. Accepting Consequences						
43. Dealing with an Accusation						
44. Negotiating						
V. Skills for Dealing with Stress						
45. Dealing with Boredom						
46. Deciding What Caused a Problem						
47. Making a Complaint						
48. Answering a Complaint						
49. Dealing with Losing						
50. Showing Sportsmanship						
51. Dealing with Being Left Out						
52. Dealing with Embarrassment						
53. Reacting to Failure						
54. Accepting No						
55. Saying No						
56. Relaxing						
57. Dealing with Group Pressure						
58. Dealing with Wanting Something That Isn't Mine						
59. Making a Decision						
60. Being Honest						

Figure 5. Student Mastery Record

Student: ____________________

Date	Skill	Role Play Participation: Main actor	Role Play Participation: Co-actor	Feedback Participation	Homework: Assigned	Homework: Completed	Rating of Skill Use in Role Play: Needs Improvement	Average	Good	Excellent
							1	2	3	4
							1	2	3	4
							1	2	3	4
							1	2	3	4
							1	2	3	4
							1	2	3	4

and then to evaluate the degree to which that objective was reached. Such definition and evaluation of behavioral objectives is implemented in Structured Learning by planning ahead of time which skills will be taught, and then by recording the level of skill attainment the student has demonstrated on the Student Mastery Record. This is particularly useful for the handicapped student who is educated in a special education program, for the Student Mastery Record can be attached to the student's Individualized Education Program (IEP) as evidence of goal attainment. Finally, the Student Mastery Record, along with the Progress Summary Sheet, may be conveniently used for tracking student progress and reassigning and regrouping into a different Structured Learning group those students whom the tracking information reveals to be misplaced.

SUMMARY

A variety of behavioral methods for screening, selecting, and grouping students for instruction in prosocial skills were examined. The components of the assessment approach that we have typically utilized with Structured Learning groups were then presented: the Student Skill Checklist, the Teacher Skill Checklist, the Skill Training Grouping Chart, the Progress Summary Sheet, and the Student Mastery Record. Once levels of skill deficiency have thus been established, we may turn—as described in the chapter that follows—to organizing the actual group, selecting its trainers, and otherwise preparing for its effective implementation.

CHAPTER 4

Beginning a Structured Learning Group

This chapter focuses on the steps that need to be taken in order to begin Structured Learning skill development instruction of skill-deficient students in a group setting. We will discuss Structured Learning in both small and large group settings, requisite student and teacher preparation designed to increase the effectiveness of Structured Learning, and the planning and organization necessary to carry out such group instruction successfully. Special emphasis is placed upon assisting teachers in providing participants with an opening framework and explanation of Structured Learning that is likely to enhance their active involvement. This chapter also includes illustrative excerpts from a beginning Structured Learning session.

Structured Learning can be carried out in both large groups (such as a non-special education classroom) and small groups of approximately five to eight students.

INSTRUCTION IN SMALL GROUPS

As noted in the preceding chapter, each Structured Learning group should consist of students who share deficiencies in specific skills or skill areas. The optimal group size for effective teaching is five to eight students and two teachers (or one teacher and a teacher's aide, student teacher, parent aide, school psychologist, counselor, or principal). Structured Learning groups tend to be active groups, and the use of two group leaders has in our experience proven highly desirable. Leaders alternate in either conducting the group's role-play procedures or attending to the students serving as role-play observers.

The students selected to participate in Structured Learning need not be from the same classroom or even from the same grade level. However, since role playing in the group more frequently leads to skilled behavior outside of the group when the role-play setting is as realistic as possible, it is often useful to include students whose social environments (family, class, peer groups) are similar. For example, selecting group participants from a common peer group will provide a shared interpersonal environment in which the students can both role play and then actually use these skills in real-life situations.

While students optimally should be grouped according to common skill deficiencies, there are situations in which such grouping is not possible. Instead, the group leaders may choose to organize their groups according to naturally occurring units, such as a classroom or residential cottage, which makes it likely that the students will have a broader range of skill strengths and weaknesses. When the groups are organized in this manner, the group leaders will initially need to target those skills in which the majority of the students show a deficit.

INSTRUCTION IN LARGE GROUPS

A classroom teacher may decide to instruct his entire class in prosocial skills for various reasons. First, his goal may be a preventive one: The teacher may want to provide his students with skill strategies and behaviors that will enable them to handle skill-relevant difficulties should they arise. A second reason for teaching prosocial skills to an entire class is to use socially competent peers as models and reinforcers for the students who have social skills deficits. If handled with sensitivity, the presence of skilled peers provides a unique advantage to the skill-deficient child. Since the effectiveness of modeling is enhanced when models are similar to the observer, a student who is proficient in a skill may be more effective as a model than the classroom teacher. A student competent in the skill can also give constructive suggestions (performance feedback) to the student struggling to master the skill, providing of course, that this is done in a friendly, caring, and encouraging manner. Children who are more adept at the skill being taught can also function effectively as co-actors in the role-play activities.

It is helpful to have two adults serve as the trainers in each large Structured Learning group, just as for smaller groups. A second adult provides assistance in presenting the initial modeling displays, coaching or guiding students through the role plays, pointing out the steps as they are modeled and acted out by the main role player, rewarding the models and role players, and providing appropriate examples of feedback. However, if another adult is unavailable, a student who is competent in the skill being taught—perhaps even one from a higher grade level—can give much of this assistance.

While it is possible to conduct modeling displays in a full class of 20 or more students, to provide sufficient opportunity for each child to assume the role of main actor (i.e., the person required to portray the skill's behavioral steps) and receive constructive feedback, it is desirable to conduct role playing in smaller groups. If two leaders are available, this may be done by dividing the larger group into two smaller groups for role playing, with one leader guiding each role-play group. Thus, the whole class would meet as a unit for the discussion of the skill and its modeling. The role play, feedback, and assignment of homework would be carried out in the smaller groups. If it is not possible to divide the larger group into smaller groups for a part of Structured Learning, a teacher can conduct Structured Learning with the entire class. Under this circumstance in particular, it is important that the group leader capture the attention and involvement of as many students as possible. This can be done by:

1. Using several students as co-actors in the role play.
2. Assigning classroom helper roles (e.g., one student at the blackboard or skills chart to point out the skill steps as they are being role played).
3. Assigning specific observer tasks to all students who are not participating actively in the role play (e.g., one row of students might watch to see if the main actor followed Step 1; another row might watch to see if she followed Step 2, and so on).

SELECTION OF GROUP LEADERS

The modeling, role-playing, and feedback activities that make up most of each Structured Learning session are a series of sequences in which behaviors are first demonstrated (modeled), rehearsed (role played), and then critiqued (feedback). This setup requires that the teacher both lead and observe, a situation in which one teacher is hard pressed to do both of these tasks well at the same time. Therefore, we recommend that each session be led by a team of two group leaders. One can usually pay special attention to the main actor, especially by helping him "set the stage" for his role play and then enact the skill's behavioral steps. While this is occurring, the second leader can attend to the other group members and help them as they observe and evaluate the unfolding role play. The two group leaders can then exchange these responsibilities on the next role play.

The group leaders conducting Structured Learning groups should have two sets of skills. The first set includes general teaching and group leadership skills, such as enthusiasm, sensitivity, and communication skills. The second set consists of skills related specifically to Structured Learning, including the following:

1. Knowledge of Structured Learning (background, procedures, goals).
2. Ability to orient both trainees and supporting staff to Structured Learning.
3. Ability to plan and present live modeling displays.
4. Ability to initiate and sustain role playing.
5. Ability to present material in concrete, behavioral form.
6. Accuracy and sensitivity in providing corrective feedback.
7. Ability to deal with group management problems in an effective manner.

INVOLVEMENT OF PARENTS

Parents should be informed of the teacher's intention to organize and conduct Structured Learning groups prior to their actual implementation. Many of the role-play situations identified by the students may depict problems that occur at home, and the students will most probably discuss with their parents the ways they are learning to deal with these problems in school. Informing parents of the goals and procedures may therefore prevent confusion and possible misunderstandings, as parents may question the relevance of working on what are in part home problems in the school setting.

Perhaps the most important reason for parental involvement is to make parents aware of Structured Learning skills and procedures so that they will be able to reinforce the child's use of the skills at home. To facilitate parents' willingness to assist in such transfer efforts, involve parents at the onset. Sending a letter to parents explaining the prosocial skills teaching goals of Structured Learning, activities in which their child will be participating (observing modeling, role playing, giving and receiving feedback, and doing homework assignments), and specific skills to be taught is one way of informing them. The teacher may also wish to invite parents to school for an orientation meeting, a more in-depth discussion of Structured Learning and suggestions on how they can help their child use these prosocial skills at home.

PHYSICAL SETTING

A specific area should be set aside for the group sessions. Chairs may be arranged in a horseshoe fashion facing a role-play area, behind which is a chalkboard or chart on which each skill's behavioral steps may be written (Figure 6). The leader and co-leader's chairs should be placed among the students' chairs to facilitate noticing appropriate and inappropriate group behaviors and to provide the necessary reinforcement or instruction to individual students. It might also be helpful for leaders to position themselves near students who tend to be restless, easily excited, or somewhat withdrawn. Maintaining close physical proximity to such students may circumvent many behavior problems before they occur.

The skill teaching setting should be furnished to resemble as much as possible the settings in which the participating students will apply the prosocial skills. This suggestion is based upon the important principle, noted earlier, for facilitating

Figure 6. Seating Chart for Group Sessions

transfer from the teaching setting to the student's real-life environment: the rule of identical elements. This rule states that the more similar or identical the two settings are, that is, the greater the number of physical and interpersonal qualities shared by them, the greater the likelihood that the student will transfer the skill from one setting to the other. Teachers can increase the degree of similarity between the classroom and other real-life settings through the creative use of available furniture and supplies. If a couch is needed for a particular role play, several chairs can be pushed together to simulate the couch; if a television set is an important part of a role play, a box, a chair, or a drawing on the chalkboard can, in imagination, approximate the real object. Of course, the actual object, or prop, should be used when it is available.

Whenever possible, Structured Learning should be carried out in the same general setting as the real-life environment of most of the participating students. When a prosocial skill is especially relevant to environments that are easily accessible, such as the school playground, cafeteria, or library, the modeling and role playing should occur in these environments. Actual and symbolic authority figures may be brought into the group to further enhance its real-life quality. For example, the teacher may request that other school personnel (e.g., the school principal) participate as co-actors when a student wishes to role play a difficult skill dealing with an authority figure.

When such real-life authorities are employed, they should either be primed to respond rewardingly to correct skill usage by the student, or at least chosen wisely so that such reward is very likely to be forthcoming even when it is not requested or prearranged with them.

GROUP FACILITATION RULES

Specific behavioral rules relevant to the smooth functioning of the skills instruction group should be decided upon prior to actually implementing the Structured Learning sessions. Such rules may include the following: (1) Wait until another person has finished talking before you begin to speak; (2) remember to keep your hands and feet to yourself; and (3) show that you are listening to others when it is their turn to talk. Four or five such group facilitation rules are a workable number with which to begin a Structured Learning group.

We urge teachers to allow students to participate in developing group facilitation rules. With some children this can be done by asking them to think of behaviors that they feel are needed for working together. Usually, however, more specific guidance must be provided, ideally in the form of leading questions, such as "What would happen if everyone talked at once?" and "How would you feel if you thought someone wasn't listening to you?" Through this method, most elementary school children will state many rules that the teachers themselves would have formulated. Allowing the group to participate in this way encourages the students' commitment to abide by these rules because they have had a part in the development of such rules.

Group rules should always define specific behaviors. A statement such as "Respect the rights of others," while being a good goal, is too abstract for many elementary-age children to understand. Instead, the students' behaviors should be clearly defined. Statements such as "Look at the person who is speaking" and "Leave toys and other objects at your desk" clearly specify behaviors in terms young children will understand.

Rules also must be phrased in a positive manner, telling students what to do, not what to avoid doing. For example, the statement "Don't talk when others are talking" should be changed to "Wait until another person has finished talking before you begin to speak."

Once group rules are established and agreed upon, it is a good idea to post them in the classroom. The rules can be reviewed at the beginning of each session until they are well-remembered by the children. Periodic review of these rules may also be needed, especially at the primary grade levels.

Establishing clearly defined rules in the early stages of group work may prevent many student behavior problems. Providing positive reinforcement for obeying the rules (e.g., "Thank you for waiting for your turn to speak") will increase the likelihood that they will be followed.

GENERAL GROUP TEACHING STRATEGIES

Kounin and Obradovic (1971) suggest certain specific teaching techniques that appear to affect the way learners behave in a classroom setting. These techniques, which relate positively to student involvement and absence of behavior problems, are particularly relevant to conducting Structured Learning groups. One such technique is *ease in transition* from one activity to another: Students are more likely to stay involved in the group's flow when the leaders move from one Structured Learning activity or component to another in a smooth and energetic manner. This may be difficult until the leader is familiar with Structured Learning; however, avoiding disjointedness and procedural confusion is a crucial factor for successfully accomplishing group work.

Another useful technique is the ability to *avoid boredom* by not overextending an activity: Group instruction should cease prior to the onset of boredom, thus maintaining interest in the activity in subsequent sessions. Including modeling, role playing, group discussion of role plays, and review of homework assignments in each group session provides a variety of activities that will help maintain student interest.

"*With-it-ness,*" or the awareness of student behavior in the group, is a very effective teacher behavior. The group leaders should be alert to students who are withdrawing from activities or those who are creating distractions for others, and implement the group management techniques described in Chapter 9 to minimize such behaviors.

Structured Learning will also be more effective if the atmosphere of the group is a positive, helping, and supportive one. *Encouragement,* rather than criticism, is characteristic of more effective learning (Larrivee, 1981). Furthermore, when an adult encourages a student, a good model for the students to emulate is provided.

Although the purpose of the Structured Learning teaching sessions is for the students to learn new, prosocial behaviors, the group also provides the *opportunity to have fun* with learning. We have found that if teachers enjoy teaching prosocial skills, their enthusiasm carries over to and is reflected in the students' level of interest.

FREQUENCY AND LENGTH OF SESSIONS

Structured Learning sessions for a given group should be held three to five times per week. They should be frequent enough that a substantial series of skills can be taught over the course of a school year, and far enough apart for children to have ample opportunity to complete their homework assignments between sessions. Sessions approximately 20 minutes long should be planned for grades one and two; 20–30 minutes for grades three and four; and 30–40 minutes for grades five and six. Of course, both the number and the length of sessions can be reduced or extended depending upon the attention span, interest, and maturity of the students. The limit of the meeting will be indicated when several children become restless and inattentive. However, because it is important to maintain the students' interest for subsequent Structured Learning sessions, sessions should be planned to end slightly before such restlessness is likely to occur. To facilitate the continued use of newly learned prosocial skills, an additional 10 minutes should be allotted at the end of every school day for students to chart the skills they have practiced during the day. This self-recording method will be discussed in Chapter 5.

REINFORCEMENT SYSTEM

In the initial stages of group work with young children, it is often helpful to implement a systematic plan for using reinforcement to help manage group members' problem behaviors and increase the likelihood of a smoothly running group. Implementation of such a plan will assist the elementary school child in learning to work in a group format, participate in role-playing activities, give appropriate feedback, and complete assigned homework.

A token system is frequently an effective means of supplying students with the positive reinforcement necessary to co-operate and work productively in a Structured Learning group setting. In one program using tokens (McGinnis, Sauerbry, & Nichols, in press), SCAMO's (Showing Caring About Myself and Others) (Figure 7) are earned for following the general group rules, participating in role plays, practicing previously learned skills in the group setting and throughout the school day, and completing individual homework assignments. These tokens, always paired with verbal praise, are given to the students on an intermittent schedule. Each day participating students chart the number of tokens they have earned. Each student is then able to spend these tokens for a variety of privileges or tangible rewards.

In the initial stages of learning, a critical rule is to give frequent positive reinforcement (Bornstein & Quevillon, 1976). In the beginning of group work, each student should earn from 5 to 10 tokens during a 30-minute session. For example, one token could be earned for coming quietly to the group; another for listening to and watching the modeling display;

Figure 7. Tokens Used in Early Group Management Activities

SCAMO

Showing Caring About Myself and Others

yet another for participating in the role play. Reinforcement also has a powerful effect if, for instance, the students who are listening are reinforced with verbal praise and tokens when one student does not appear to be paying attention. This creates a ripple effect (Kounin, 1977), and the inattentive student will most likely begin to listen. This strategy allows the group leader to control the group in a positive, helping way, rather than "nagging" a student to pay attention. Other useful rules for implementing an effective token economy with handicapped children are described in detail by Walker (1979).

TEACHER PREPARATION

Those who will be implementing Structured Learning groups must take the steps previously described prior to carrying out the actual Structured Learning instruction with students. Such careful preplanning will provide a structure that fosters a positive learning environment. The checklist in Figure 8 is a guide for the preplanning that has been described.

Figure 8. Teacher Preparation Checklist

_____ An area of the classroom is available and ready for conducting the group (space for chairs, large chart, blackboard, etc.).

_____ The time of day the group will meet is scheduled and the length of the sessions is estimated.

_____ The group leaders are prepared in their knowledge of Structured Learning.

_____ Parents and others (e.g., other teachers, principal) are informed of the goals and strategies that will be used.

_____ A Teacher Skill Checklist (Chapter 3) has been completed on each selected participant.

_____ (Optional) Each student participant has completed the Student Skill Checklist.

_____ Group rules are established with the group's assistance.

_____ The reinforcement plan is established and explained to the students.

PREPARATION SESSION WITH
STRUCTURED LEARNING PARTICIPANTS

Conducting a preparation session with the students who will be participating, either as a separate group meeting or as part of the initial Structured Learning session itself, is helpful in order to heighten the students' motivation to attend and participate in the group as well as to provide them with accurate expectations of what the group's activities will be like. This session should include (1) introducing group leaders and participants, (2) explaining what prosocial skills are, (3) presenting an overview of Structured Learning procedures, (4) establishing group rules, and (5) explaining the reinforcement system. It is especially important during the course of this preparatory presentation and discussion to involve the children themselves. The leaders' goal here must be to encourage in each student a sense of personal relevance and involvement in Structured Learning. Ideally, in this session students will develop a belief that Structured Learning participation can help them learn things *they* want to learn and need to learn. Such a goal is more likely to be reached if the leader presents much of the information in skill-relevant terms, and also involves the students in discussion of shared skill deficits and their implications.

The following outline illustrates such a preparation session with skill-deficient children.

A. Introductions
   1. Introduce yourselves if you are not known by the students.
   2. Ask the students to introduce themselves. During this time you can ask for some additional information as a way of breaking the ice.
   Examples:—"How about if we go around the group, and each person says his or her name and one thing he or she likes (and dislikes) about school."
   —"Why don't you tell us your name and one activity you like outside of school."
B. Explanation of prosocial skills
   1. List examples of prosocial skills.
   2. Ask the students to provide other examples of prosocial skills.
   Example:

   Teacher: What we're going to do first of all is explain to you what we will be doing in our group. We'll be working on social skills, also called people skills. What I mean by social skills are things like listening to other people, asking questions in a friendly way, asking favors of others, and sharing. We'll work on ways to deal with your feelings, like when you are angry or upset, and ways to stay out of trouble, such as how to stay out of fights. Can you think of other social skills?

Steve: Behave in class.

Teacher: What do you mean by behaving in class?

Steve: Like when you yell.

Teacher: Okay. When do you yell in class?

Steve: When I get mad.

Teacher: So a social skill would be how to deal with being mad or upset. Is that a social skill you'd like to work on?

Steve: Yeah.

Teacher: Good. Who can think of other social skills?

(No response)

Teacher: What about on the playground. Are there any playground problems that you have or that you have seen?

Bill: Outside kids pick on me and call me names.

Teacher: So it's difficult for you to deal with somebody calling you names?

Bill: Yes.

Teacher: How to deal with somebody calling you names or teasing you is a good social skill. Thank you, Bill.

Susan: Minding your manners is one.

Teacher: Susan, tell me one thing you do when you show your manners.

Susan: Well . . . say thank you.

Teacher: Yes, that's a good social skill.

Tim: When somebody walks by, I try to trip them.

Teacher: So a social skill might be how to get attention in a good way, rather than tripping someone. Tim, is that what you mean?

Tim:	Yeah.
Teacher:	That's a good social skill to work on.
Lori:	My sister takes pine cones off trees and throws them at people.
Teacher:	So a social skill you'd like to work on is what to do when someone does something they shouldn't?
Lori:	Yeah. I go tell my mom.
Teacher:	That's one way of handling the problem. We're going to be talking about lots of other ways to deal with problems like this. You have named some very good social skills. We'll show you the way to do some social skills. Then we'll ask you to try them in the group and then try them on your own.

C. Overview of Structured Learning
   1. Provide the students with an explanation of the *purpose* of the group sessions.
   Examples:—"We'll be working on ways to get along with others."
            —"We'll be practicing ways to stay out of trouble."
            —"We'll be teaching you some things to make it easier for you to make friends."
            —"We'll be practicing ways to talk to adults and others who don't seem to understand you."
   2. Describe the four basic Structured Learning procedures for acquiring prosocial skills.
   Examples:—"First, we'll show you the way to do it." (modeling)
            —"Then, you'll try it." (role playing)
            —"Then, we'll talk about what you did well and some things you could do to make it even better." (performance feedback)
            —"Then, you'll have the opportunity to practice the skill." (transfer of training)
   3. Further describe the Structured Learning procedures by comparing them to the manner in which any new game or sport is learned.
   Examples:—"What are the steps in learning to play volleyball?"
            —"What do you do first? Second?" (etc.)
            —"Okay, the first thing is to know how to hit the ball. How do you learn to do that?" (First you watch someone do it; then you try it; people give you suggestions to help you do it better; then you practice hitting the ball on your own.)

4. Involve the group members in talking about a prosocial skill. Ask the group what parts (or steps) there are to listening to someone, for example. (Emphasize the behaviors that *show* another person that you are listening to him.)

Examples:—"When someone starts talking, what do you do first to let him know you heard him?"

—"Right! You look at the person. What do you do next?"

D. Establishment of group rules or "Helpful Reminders"
Example:

Teacher:	In this group, we want to encourage and help each other. There are some things we can all do that will be helpful to each other. Let's come up with a list of helpful things we can do and I'll list them on the chalkboard. Who can think of one way?
	(No response)
Teacher:	What if one person is talking and someone else starts to talk at the same time? Is that a good thing to do?
Group:	No, uh-uh.
Teacher:	What would be a Helpful Reminder about that?
Bill:	Wait your turn instead of just starting to talk.
Teacher:	Good. Why should you wait your turn instead of just starting to talk?
Shane:	'Cause everyone would be interrupting everyone else.
Teacher:	Right. Would "Wait your turn to talk" be a Helpful Reminder for our group?
	(Group members nod yes.)
Teacher:	Tom, you remembered our very first reminder . . . you waited until I was finished before you let me know you were ready to say something. Do you have an idea?
Tom:	Accept what somebody says.
Teacher:	Okay! How could you show that you accept what somebody says?
Steve:	Don't talk . . . and don't laugh at them.
Teacher:	Good. Could we include those under listening?

Steve:	Yeah.
Teacher:	So, if you're listening, you're remembering not to laugh or talk when somebody is talking. What else?
Michelle:	You look at them.
Teacher:	Good, Michelle.
Michelle:	We had this place where kids go when they lose control.
Teacher:	So, when someone gets upset in the group, you think it would be a good idea to have some place for that person to go?
Michelle:	That could be a reminder.
Teacher:	So the reminder would be when you're really upset or don't feel you can handle the group, you can say you need to leave? Who should you tell?
Tom:	The teacher.
Teacher:	Okay, if you think you have to leave, you'll need to tell me. I think that's a good reminder. What do you think?

(Group members nod yes.)

Teacher:	We're sitting really close to each other. It might be easy to forget not to bother somebody. That could get someone upset if they're trying to listen. Should we have a reminder about that? Steve.
Steve:	Keep your hands and feet to yourself.
Teacher:	Great! That's a nice way of saying it. Thank you, Steve. Does everyone agree with that one?
Bobby:	Some kids play with toys during reading group and Mr. _____ gets mad.
Teacher:	Why do you think Mr. _____ gets mad or upset at this?
Bobby:	'Cause we want to play with the toys, too, I guess.
Teacher:	So it's difficult for you to read when someone is playing with toys?
Bobby:	Yes.
Michelle:	Kids shouldn't have toys in our group.

Teacher: Bobby and Michelle feel that we shouldn't bring toys or things that will distract us to our group. Would that be a Helpful Reminder?

(The group agrees.)

Teacher: How about if we say it like this: "Remember to leave toys and other things at your desk"?

(The group agrees.)

Teacher: You came up with some great Helpful Reminders for our group. All right. We have five reminders. If we get too many, it will be difficult to remember them all. I'll copy these onto a chart and hang it on the wall. That way they'll be here if anyone needs to look and see what the reminders are. (See Figure 9.)

E. Explanation of the reinforcement system
    1. Explain what tokens the students will receive.
    Example:— "These cards are SCAMOs. They stand for 'Showing Caring About Myself and Others.' You can earn these."
    2. Explain when, or for what behavior, they can earn a token.
    Examples:—"You can earn a SCAMO for following the Helpful Reminders, participating in the group, and practicing the skills we work on."
            —"A rule is, however, that I get to give out the SCAMOs. And I get to decide when you have earned them. For example, you may not get a SCAMO each time you follow the rules or participate, only sometimes."

Figure 9. Chart of Helpful Reminders

Helpful Reminders

Wait your turn to talk.

Listen to others (look at them, remember not to laugh or talk).

If you get upset, you can say that you want to leave the group for a while.

Keep your hands and feet to yourself.

Remember to leave toys and other things at your desk.

3. Explain what the tokens can be exchanged for.

Example:— "At the end of the group, you'll count your SCAMOs and write the number on the chart by your name. Then you can exchange the SCAMOs for these activities." (Students are shown a list of activities with their corresponding token costs.)

4. Explain when the tokens can be exchanged.

Example:— "You can exchange your points for activities when you finish your reading assignment, and again during the last 15 minutes of the day."

SUMMARY

This chapter has described the procedures necessary to organize and begin effective Structured Learning groups. Teacher preparation, student preparation, and the procedures involved in an initial group session have been discussed. The next chapter focuses on the implementation of Structured Learning components (modeling, role playing, feedback, and transfer of training) in Structured Learning groups with skill-deficient children.

CHAPTER 5

Conducting a
Structured Learning Group

The present chapter will provide the reader with specific and detailed instructions for the actual implementation of Structured Learning. This includes enhancing student motivation, formulating behavioral skill steps with the students (see Chapter 6 for detailed lists of skill steps), and implementing the four components of Structured Learning (modeling, role playing, performance feedback, and transfer of training).

ENHANCING STUDENT MOTIVATION

Student motivation for productive participation in Structured Learning is likely to be enhanced by where and when the group meets, and by whom it is conducted. While transfer-relevant considerations (i.e., identical elements in group and real-life settings) should remain the primary determinant of where the group meets, students will sometimes be more eager participants if the session is held in a special place, a place in which it is, in a sense, a privilege to be. This may be the teacher's lounge, a conference room, or some other usually off-limits school room or area. When shall the group meet? It is helpful for motivation enhancement purposes if the Structured Learning session is scheduled at a time when participating students, in order to attend, will not have to miss an activity or class that they especially enjoy. On the contrary, if attending the session gets them out of something that they dislike, motivation for Structured Learning participation is likely to be correspondingly heightened. Who shall lead the group? Schools, like all institutions, often have very effective grapevines through which communications—including how good or bad a new activity is—pass very rapidly. Therefore, the first Structured Learning sessions of the first group organized in any school can be an especially potent influence upon whether or not a large number of students are motivated to "get into it." We urge that the best available leaders be utilized for a school's first use of Structured Learning.

Most students are more likely to be willing participants in Structured Learning when they feel the need to learn the skills presented. Since a discussion of prosocial skills will have preceded the first group session, the students should have an idea of the type of skills they will be learning. Therefore, it is especially helpful, in the first session, to request that students generate a list of skills that *they* would like to learn. Some students, at first, may be reluctant to openly mention problems they are experiencing, and consequently what skills they want or need to learn. However, other skill-deficient students may not feel threatened at all about sharing this type of information. When a few students reveal their perceived skill needs, others in the group will also be likely to share theirs.

EXAMPLE

"Remember yesterday when we discussed different people skills? This group came up with many excellent examples of such skills. Now, we want to decide on the skills we will start working on. Let's list these skills on the chalkboard."

If there is little response from the students in the group, the teacher may need to lead the group in a more directive way.

EXAMPLES

"Someone mentioned that he seemed to always be getting into trouble in math class—the math teacher was upset that this person didn't seem to be listening. What skill could help this person out?"

"How many of you find it difficult to complete your school assignments? Is this a good skill to work on?"

"Last week somebody mentioned to me that she was being teased on the playground. Raise your hand if being teased is a problem for you that you'd like to work on."

Once a list of such skills is formulated, one skill is chosen for instruction. If the skill Listening is included in the children's list, it is often an excellent skill with which to begin instruction for any grade level. Others from the first skill group, Classroom Survival Skills, are also good skills with which to begin. However, if the majority of the group is having, for example, playground problems due to not handling being teased in an appropriate manner, Responding to Teasing should be selected early in the group's sessions. While it is thus crucial that skills selected be those that participating students *want* to learn, it is also important that the students *successfully* use the prosocial skill in the beginning stages. Using the skill must provide more reinforcement to the students than the reinforcement received from their previous patterns of behavior. Therefore, if it is unlikely that students will initially be able to deal with an emotionally laden situation (such as being teased), it would be better to begin instruction on a skill they are likely to have success in performing. In addition, learning a skill that the students will have the opportunity to use within the group leader's view will allow the leader to reinforce students for use of the skill.

In summary, the group leader should follow these guidelines for enhancing student motivation:

1. Take into account motivational considerations in deciding where and when to meet and by whom the group will be led.
2. Choose skills relevant to the needs of the students as *they* perceive their needs.
3. In selecting the initial skills to be taught, choose ones with which the students are likely to be successful.
4. Provide students with reinforcement (e.g., tokens, praise) when the skill is used successfully.

FORMULATING THE SKILL STEPS

Once the first skill is chosen, the students should be asked to help determine the specific behavioral steps that make up this skill. For example, if Listening is the skill being taught, the students should be asked something like "What do you do to show someone that you're listening to them?"; or, for the skill of Joining In, "What is the first thing that you do when you want to join in an ongoing activity?" Although the leader will be aware of the behavioral steps to achieve the skill (as presented in Chapter 6), the students' input is crucial at this stage. Their participation in formulating these behavioral steps will serve to enhance their commitment to learning the specific skill. In addition, it will help assure that the steps are phrased in vocabulary easily understood by the group, thus facilitating memorization.

If the students are reluctant to respond to general, open-ended questions like the examples just presented, it may again be necessary to lead them in a more directive manner.

EXAMPLE

Teacher:	I'm going to listen to someone telling a story and I want you to watch and see what I do. Tommy, will you tell me what you did after school last night?
Tommy:	I rode the bus home and then watched T.V.
Teacher:	(Sits quietly and watches Tommy.) What did you watch on T.V.?
Tommy:	(Explains a program he saw on television.)
Teacher:	(Nods head; says "uh-huh.")
	(Tommy finishes his story.)
	Tommy, thank you for sharing that story with us. (Looks around the group.) Did I seem to be listening to Tommy?
	(Group members reply yes and nod.)
	What did I do to show Tommy that I was listening to him?

At this time, the students will most likely report many of the behaviors the teacher exhibited. If not, the teacher should further lead the group with questions such as "Did I look at Tommy or did I look away from him?" and "Was I sitting quietly or was I turning around in my chair?"

Once the steps to the skill are agreed upon, using the behavioral skill steps in Chapter 6 as a guide, these steps should be listed on a chart and displayed so that every child is able to refer to them. (The steps can initially be written on the chalkboard and then later transferred to a chart.) Thus, the guidelines for formulating skill steps are as follows:

1. List the title of the skill.
2. Guide students into formulating the behavioral steps to the skill (use the skill steps presented in Chapter 6 as a guide).
3. Post a chart of the skill and its corresponding steps so that students can easily refer to the steps.

COMPONENTS OF STRUCTURED LEARNING

MODELING

Modeling is the first Structured Learning procedure and is designed to show the participating students *what* to do. The modeling displays presented to the students should demonstrate the behavioral steps that make up a given skill in a clear and unambiguous way. All of the steps making up the skill should be modeled, in the correct sequence. Generally, the modeling will consist of live vignettes enacted by the two group leaders. When a second group leader is not available, however, a reasonably skillful student may serve as a model along with the teacher. In all instances it is especially important to rehearse the vignettes carefully prior to class, making sure that all of the skill's steps are enacted correctly and in the proper sequence.

The group leaders should plan their modeling displays carefully. The content of these displays should be relevant to the life situations of the students in the Structured Learning group. Appropriate content for these modeling displays can be selected from the Student Skill Checklist or the Problem Situation descriptions on the Teacher Skill Checklist (Chapter 3), the general, preparatory discussion of Structured Learning (Chapter 4), or the suggested situations for enactment of each skill (Chapter 6).

EXAMPLE

"Listening during math class is a problem we discussed earlier. I am going to be the teacher, Mr. _____, and show you how to add two numerals. Ms. _____ will be the student. I want you to watch and see if Ms. _____ follows our steps to listening."

In order to help students attend to the modeled skill enactments, direct them to the skill chart on which the name of the skill being taught and its behavioral steps are listed. Tell students to watch and listen closely as the models portray the skill. Particular care should be given to helping students identify the behavioral steps as they are presented in the context of the modeling display. Selecting individual students to watch for each given step is another way of encouraging attention to the modeling vignette.

EXAMPLE

"What is the first step to showing that you are listening? Bill. (Bill reads or recites Step 1.) Good. Now, we need to watch and see if Ms. _____ follows Step 1. Michelle, will you watch for us?"

Modeling is also more effective when a coping model is presented as opposed to a mastery model (Bandura, 1977). For example, if the model's task is to demonstrate the skill of Responding to Teasing, it is more effective if the model first "struggles" with walking away from her tormentor. Walking away slowly, with teeth clenched, will show that this is not an easy task to accomplish. Modeling verbal mediation, for instance, saying aloud, "It's hard to walk away, but I can do it," further helps to demonstrate a coping model. This provides a more realistic modeling display than simply walking away devoid of any apparent emotion or conflict.

It is extremely valuable and necessary that models (and role players) practice verbal mediation during the modeling (or role playing) in order to demonstrate the cognitive process that underlies skill performance. Saying the steps aloud as they are performing the behaviors will also facilitate learning. When modeling the skill of Listening in the context previously described, for instance, the model might say, "I have to listen to the teacher. I don't understand this math very well, and it's hard to listen, but I just have to. What's the first step? Okay, look at the person," and so on. In another example of the use of verbal mediation in modeling a skill (Responding to Teasing), the model recites the steps of the skill in the context of the situation. The model might say something like "I believe I am being teased because they are looking at me and laughing. I don't like to be teased, but I won't let them know that! I'm angry, so first I have to cool down. I need to count to five. One . . . two . . . three . . . four . . . five. Okay, now I think of my choices," etc. This accompanying narration increases the effectiveness of the modeling display by modeling the cognitive process one goes through in performing the skill (Bandura, 1977) and also may facilitate the generalization of the skill (Stokes & Baer, 1977). Many students will likely need to be taught the process of thinking aloud. For young children, in particular, it is likely to prove helpful to have them practice thinking aloud while doing other types of activities, for example, "I pick up the scissors and cut along the lines. I keep cutting. Go slow. Keep cutting. There! I cut the animal out. Now I paste it on the paper." Other activities useful in teaching primary-age children to think aloud can be found in the *Think Aloud* program developed by Camp and Bash (1981).

At least two examples of the skill should be modeled so that the students are exposed to use of the skill in different situations. For example, it may be important for Todd to learn how to join in a volleyball game at school recess, but he also needs to see that he can use the same skill for asking to join a reading activity in the classroom or a baseball game with peers in his own neighborhood. Thus, two or more content areas should be depicted for each skill.

Group leaders usually do not have to prepare full scripts for the modeling displays. Instead, they can plan their roles and likely responses in outline form in their preclass preparations. As stated previously, it is very important that the situations chosen for these displays depict or at least approximate the students' real-life situations or needs. The modeling display outlines should incorporate the following guidelines:

1. At least two examples for each demonstration of a skill should be used. Since a single skill will most often be used in more than one group session, more than two modeling displays will often have to be developed.

2. Situations that are relevant to the students' real-life circumstances should be selected.

3. The person enacting the skill's behavioral steps should be portrayed as a child reasonably similar in age, socioeconomic background, verbal ability, and other salient characteristics to the children in the Structured Learning group.

4. All displays should depict positive outcomes.

5. The model who has used the skill correctly should receive reinforcement within the context of the modeling display in the form of praise or a desired outcome.

6. All modeling displays should demonstrate all the behavioral steps of the skill being modeled, in the correct sequence.

7. Modeling displays should depict only one skill at a time. All extraneous content should be eliminated.

8. The model should "think aloud" those steps that ordinarily would be thought silently.

ROLE PLAYING

Following the modeling display, discussion should focus on relating the modeled skill to the lives of the students. The group leaders should request comments on the way the steps portrayed could be applied in real-life situations encountered by the children. It is most helpful to have students focus on how they might use the skill now and in the future, rather than relating the skill to past events. Role playing in Structured Learning is intended to serve as behavioral rehearsal or practice for future use of the skill. Therefore, the group leaders need to be aware that role playing past events, if they do not have relevance for future situations, is of limited value. However, discussion of past events involving use of the skill can be useful in stimulating the students to think of times when a similar situation may occur in the future. In such a case, the hypothetical future situation, rather than a reenactment of the past event, would be selected for role playing.

Role playing, the second Structured Learning component, helps the student learn *how* to perform the skill. First, a student describes a situation in his own life in which skill usage might be helpful. That student is then designated as the main actor. The main actor then chooses a second student (or one of the group leaders) to play the role of the significant other person (e.g., parent, peer, sibling, teacher) in his life who is relevant to the skill problem. It is important that the student choose as a co-actor someone who resembles the real-life person in as many ways as possible. The leader then elicits from the main actor any additional information necessary to set the stage for the role play. In order to make the role play as realistic as possible, the leader should obtain descriptions of the physical setting in which use of the skill is likely to occur, the events that precede the problem, the other person's mood or manner, and any other relevant information.

Before beginning the actual role play, the group leader should review each skill step as it applies to the role-play situation, thus assisting the main actor in making a successful effort. It is crucial that the main actor attempt to enact the behavioral steps that have been modeled; this is the main purpose of the role play. The main actor should be directed to refer to the skill chart on which the behavioral steps are shown, and instructed to talk himself through the skill while role playing. Research (e.g., Camp & Bash, 1981) suggests that this verbal mediation (talking aloud) in the role-play setting helps to restrain impulsivity and assists the student's retention and organization of the behaviors. As the group leader reviews skill steps with the main actor, he may find it useful to rehearse with the student what to say and do during the role play to illustrate each step. The leader should ask questions such as "What could you say for Step 1?" If the student is uncertain of how to respond, a more directive question should be asked.

Before the role play begins, the group leaders need to remind all of the participants of their roles and responsibilities: The main actor is to follow the behavioral steps; the co-actor is to stay in the role of the other person; and the observers are to watch carefully for the performance of the behavioral steps (the leader may request, as in the modeling displays, that individual students watch for the use of particular behavioral steps). For the first several role plays the participants can be coached regarding the types of cues to observe (e.g., facial expression, posture, tone of voice, content of speech). The role players are then instructed to begin the role play.

At this point, it is the main responsibility of the leaders to provide the main actor with whatever help or coaching he needs in order to keep the role play going according to the behavioral steps. Students who "break role" and begin to explain their behavior or make comments that are not part of their role should be encouraged to return to the role and make these explanations at a later time. If the role play is clearly going astray from the behavioral steps in any other way, the scene can be stopped, needed instruction can be provided, and then the role play can be recommenced, beginning again with the skill's first behavioral step. One leader should be positioned near the chalkboard or the skills chart to point to each of the behavioral steps, in turn, as the role play unfolds. This will assist the main actor (as well as the other group participants) in following each of these steps in order. The guidelines that follow describe the factors that must be attended to when conducting role plays:

1. A student describes the situation in which the skill may be helpful.
2. The student chooses a co-actor, one who reminds him most of the person with whom he has the problem.

3. Relevant information surrounding the real event is presented (description of the physical setting, of events preceding the problem, and of the manner of the person with whom the problem occurs).
4. Skill steps are reviewed and the main actor is directed to look at the skill chart which displays these steps.
5. The main actor is directed to "think out loud."
6. The responsibilities of all the participants are designated.
7. One group leader assists the main actor (assistance includes pointing to each behavioral step on the chart as the role play is carried out); the other group leader sits with the members of the group observing the role play and keeps them on track.

Here is an example of a role play from start to finish.

Skill 10: Ignoring Distractions
1. Count to five.
2. Say to yourself "I won't look. I'll keep on working."
3. Continue to work.
4. Say to yourself "Good for me. I did it!"

Preparation
1. Michelle stated that it was very difficult for her to ignore distractions during reading class. She frequently must stay after school because of her behavior during this class and therefore she wants to role play the skill of Ignoring Distractions, which has just been modeled.
2. Michelle chooses one of the group leaders, Mr. Harris, as the person who reminds her most of her reading teacher, Mr. Jones.
3. The classroom is set up to resemble Michelle's reading class (the chairs are placed in a semi-circle in front of the chalkboard). Michelle has stated that the noise of other students talking in the reading group distracts her and keeps her from concentrating on what the teacher is saying to the group. Two students are then requested to read aloud from their reading books as soon as the role play begins. Michelle describes the characteristics of her reading teacher (he looks sharply at her when she turns around in her chair; he has a deep voice).
4. The skill steps are reviewed and Michelle is directed to look at the chart displaying these steps.
5. Michelle is directed to do her thinking out loud.
6. Remaining group participants are each selected to watch whether Michelle follows particular skill steps. The group

participants are also asked to observe Michelle's nonverbal behavior and whether or not she shows her frustration (e.g., facial expressions, body posture).

7. Since one group leader has been chosen to participate in the role play, the other leader will assist Michelle in the role play as well as attempt to keep remaining group members paying attention.

Role Play

Michelle is seated at her desk and the teacher (Mr. Harris) begins instruction on the short vowel sounds. The two students selected to create distractions are sitting in the semi-circle (reading group) and begin taking turns reading aloud.

Michelle: It's hard to think! But I have to . . . Okay, the first step is counting to five. One . . . two . . . three . . . four . . . five.

(The leader moves her hand to the second step on the chart. Michelle makes no response and turns to look at the students who are reading.)

Mr. Harris: (Glares at Michelle.) Michelle, please pay attention!
(Jones)

Leader: Michelle, you did great on the first step. You counted to five. What is the second step?

Michelle: I can think about what the teacher is saying. I'll keep looking at the teacher. (Michelle turns back to face the reading teacher.)

Leader: Right. Now, let's start the role play again. Readers, go back to the beginning of your story. Mr. Harris, please begin your instruction again. Ready, Michelle?

Michelle: I can think about what Mr. Jones is saying. It's hard. First I count to five. One . . . two . . . three . . . four . . . five. Now I keep looking at Mr. Jones.

(As the role play continues, Michelle at one point starts to turn around. The leader quickly places her hand at Step 3.)

Michelle: I can keep listening . . . I can do it.

(When a few minutes have passed, the teacher [Mr. Harris] instructs the students to open their reading books.)

Leader: (Points to Step 4.)

Michelle: "Good for me! I did it!"

Role playing scenes such as the one just described should be continued until all students have had an opportunity to participate as the main actor at least once. Usually this will require more than one session for a given skill. We suggest that each session begin with two (preferably new) modeling vignettes for the chosen skill, even if the skill is not new to the group. It is important to note that while the framework (behavioral skill steps) of each role play remains the same, the actual content can and should change from role play to role play. It is the problem as it actually occurs, or could occur, in each student's real-life environment that should be the content of that child's role play. Additionally, role playing the skill a number of times, with different people, and in a variety of staged settings and hypothetical situations (rearranging room furniture and adding props) will increase the likelihood that the student will use the skill in places other than the teaching setting (Stokes & Baer, 1977).

One type of situation in which it is preferable for a leader to assume the co-actor role is when inappropriate behaviors must be enacted as part of the role-play situation, as required in role playing the skill of Responding to Teasing. A student should never be placed in the position of exhibiting inappropriate behaviors even when the goal is to create a realistic role-play situation. We have found that, far too often, the students enjoy the part of tormentors, and this is easily carried too far, with the main point of the role play being lost. In addition, we do not want students to act in the role-play setting in ways we do not want them to act in real-life settings. It is also beneficial to have the leader participate as the co-actor when it is crucial to have an adult role realistically portrayed, such as in Michelle's case. Leaders as co-actors may also be particularly helpful when dealing with less verbal or more hesitant role players.

PERFORMANCE FEEDBACK

A brief feedback period follows each role play. This helps the main actor find out how well he followed the behavioral steps, assesses the impact of the role play on the co-actor, and provides the main actor with encouragement to try the skill in real life. To implement the feedback process, the leader should ask the main actor to listen to others' comments before responding to them or evaluating his own performance. In this way he can learn to evaluate the effectiveness of his skill performance in light of evidence from others.

The co-actor is asked about her reactions first. Next the observers comment on how well the main actor performed the skill. The students who were assigned to watch for each specific skill step should first report on whether or not each step was followed and how. Then the other students can offer their comments about performance of these steps or other relevant aspects of the role play. Suggestions for what the role player could do to be more successful, constructive reminders to include a specific skill step, and comments pertaining to the feelings of the role players or to the consistency of the role player's body language with his verbal comments are examples of acceptable feedback from the observers. Encouraging group members to participate in feedback also focuses their attention on the role playing and assists in preventing boredom and potential behavior problems.

Next, the leaders should comment in particular on how well the behavioral steps were followed and provide social reinforcement (praise, approval, encouragement) for close following. Although it is desirable to have the observers evaluate the main actor's role play prior to the leader's responses, if much negative feedback and many unconstructive responses result, the order should be reversed. If this is necessary, it is an indication that appropriate and helpful feedback needs to be modeled for the group participants. Another method of encouraging positive, helpful, and constructive feedback suggestions in the initial stages of Structured Learning is to state that only positive feedback can be given from the students, and the criticism, along with additional praise, will be given by the group leaders. Once the group's focus is on the main actor's positive behaviors and constructive criticism has been modeled by the leaders for a period of time, eliciting both positive feedback and constructive criticism from the students prior to presenting the leader's feedback can be resumed.

Several of the skills presented (see Chapter 6) require the

students to "think of your choices." The only way that the observers will be sure that this step was followed is for the leader to encourage the main actor to think out loud. The observer should then be asked, "How do you know this step was followed?"; the observer's response will be something like "Because she named her choices" or "She said she was thinking." Because Structured Learning is a behavioral approach, the feedback given regarding whether or not a step was performed should focus on overt behaviors (i.e., "She said _____," "She did _____"), not broad evaluative criticism. Questions such as "How do you know?" or "What did she do?" will emphasize this behavioral focus, and teach observers to provide concrete evidence to back up their feedback.

The observers should be instructed to pay particular attention to the main actor's nonverbal cues or body language. If the main actor has said that he was upset, yet he was smiling, the incongruity should be brought to his attention. The participants must learn that nonverbal language often conveys more to the observer than what is actually spoken. Asking the questions previously suggested will also emphasize the importance of nonverbal language. For example, the observer can be asked, "How do you know she asked the question in a friendly way?" The observer's response might be "She smiled" or "She looked relaxed."

The use of reinforcement plays a critical role in Structured Learning groups. Students should be reinforced with tokens or points and praise for their participation in the role play and feedback activities. To be most effective in their use of reinforcement, teachers should adhere to the following guidelines:

1. Provide reinforcement only after role plays that follow the behavioral steps.
2. Provide reinforcement at the earliest appropriate opportunity after the role plays.
3. Provide reinforcement to the co-actor for being helpful and cooperative.
4. Praise particular aspects of performance, for example, "That's a nice way to say it" or "You used a nice, friendly tone of voice."

5. Provide enough role-play activities for each group member to have sufficient opportunity to be reinforced.
6. Provide reinforcement in an amount consistent with the quality of the role play.
7. Provide no reinforcement when the role play departs significantly from the behavioral steps (except for trying in the initial stages of Structured Learning).
8. Provide reinforcement for an individual's improvement over a previous performance.

After hearing all the feedback, the main actor is invited to comment on the role play. Cartledge and Milburn (1980) offer examples of questions that can be asked of the main actor to encourage such self-evaluation:

Skill 38: Responding to Teasing
What did you want to happen?
Did they stop teasing you?
What else did they do?
Were you pleased with the way you got them to stop?
  (Or why do you think they didn't stop?)
If you were being teased again, would you do the same thing?
What would you try to do better?
How do you think the boys feel?
What will you do the next time you meet these boys? (p. 75)

In all aspects of feedback, it is very important that the teacher or other group leader maintain the behavioral focus of Structured Learning. The teacher's comments must be directed to the presence or absence of specific, concrete behaviors and not take the form of general, evaluative comments. Feedback, of course, may be positive or negative in content. Negative comments should always be followed by a constructive comment as to how a particular skill or skill step might be improved. At minimum, a poor performance (major departures from the behavioral steps) can be praised as "a good try," and then the skill should be retaught or the students should be guided through the skill performance. Students failing to follow the relevant behavioral steps in their role play should be given the opportunity to role play these same behavioral steps again after receiving corrective feedback, reteaching, or direct guidance. It is critical that the student be successful in his skill performance. As a further feedback procedure, the role plays can be audiotaped or videotaped. Giving the students opportunities to observe themselves on tape can be an effective aid, enabling them to reflect on their own behavior.

Since a primary goal of Structured Learning is skill flexibility, role plays that depart somewhat from the behavioral steps selected may not be "wrong." That is, a different approach to the skill may in fact "work" in some situations. Teachers should stress to students that they are trying to teach effective alternatives to be included in the student's repertoire of skill behaviors, not the "one true way" to build and use a skill. It may be appropriate from time to time to add, drop, or alter the behavioral steps of any given skill depending on the main actor and, especially, the situation in which he plans to use the skill in real life.

TRANSFER OF TRAINING

Several aspects of the teaching sessions previously described are designed to increase the likelihood that learning in the teaching setting will transfer to students' real-life environments. We suggest, however, that even more steps be taken to maximize transfer. Transfer of training is, in a way, the most important Structured Learning component. Several studies indicate that although Structured Learning is a successful strategy for effecting skill acquisition, these behaviors may not be maintained over time or generalize outside of the teaching setting unless specific techniques are implemented to assist this transfer (Goldstein, 1981). Walker (1979) views changes in behavior as a two-stage process. Stage One consists of strategies to change the behavior. Stage Two consists of a second set of strategies to assure that the learned behavior is applied over time, under a variety of conditions, and in other environments. Thus, our teaching must not overlook this second, critical aspect of instruction.

Homework Assignments

We have found the use of homework assignments as a transfer-enhancing procedure to be particularly successful with Structured Learning groups. In this procedure students are instructed to try in their own real-life settings the behaviors they have practiced during the teaching session. It is useful to start with relatively simple homework behaviors and, as mastery is achieved, work up to more complex and demanding assignments. This provides the teacher with an opportunity to reinforce each approximation to real-life skill usage. The student should not be expected to perform the skill *perfectly* when first using it in real-life contexts. Reinforcement should be given as the student's performance becomes more and more like ideal skill performance. In this regard, it is important to note that successful experiences at beginning homework assignments are crucial in encouraging the student to make further attempts at real-life skill use.

Homework assignments are given to those students who have role played a given skill as main actors. Homework assignments begin with the teacher and student together deciding when and how the student will use the skill, and progress to the stage where the student herself records the skills she has used. One of four stages of homework can be used, depending upon the level of the student's mastery of a particular skill. It is most beneficial, however, to begin the assignment of homework for each skill with the first stage (Homework 1) and gradually progress to the more student-independent level of the fourth stage.

Homework 1. The students think of situations (either at home or school) in which they would like to or feel they need to practice the skill. It is especially useful if the situation they choose is the same one they have role played. On the homework sheet, the student or the teacher lists the student's name and the date the assignment is made, along with the title of the skill the student will practice and its behavioral steps. Together, the teacher and the student decide on the person with whom the student will try the skill and when she will actually make the attempt (e.g., during math class, at recess, at home during dinner), and enter these decisions on the Homework 1 report. After the student actually practices the skill, she will write on the report what happened when she tried the skill. The student then evaluates her use of the skill (or how well she followed the behavioral steps) by circling one of the faces that serve as ratings for this self-evaluation (☺ = I performed the steps well; ☺ = I did okay, but could have done better; or ☹ = I had trouble following the steps) and gives a reason for this self-evaluation (e.g., I tried all of the steps, or I forgot a step). It must be made clear to the students that this evaluation pertains to how well they carried out the skill steps, rather than how well the skill actually worked. A completed Homework 1 assignment is shown in Figure 10, while a blank form is provided in Figure 11.

Homework 2 (Red Flag). In preparation for this assignment, the student should write his name and the date the assignment is given on the Red Flag homework sheet. He (or the teacher) should also enter the title of the skill along with the behavioral steps that constitute the skill. The student is then told that he will be "set up." For example, if the skill is Asking for Help, the student should be told something like "During math this morning, I will give you work that you won't understand. I want you to remember the skill steps. They are on your home-work sheet. Remember, I will be setting you up. It's a Red Flag!" (Hawkins, Note 4). When the teacher has given the difficult assignment to the student and he has reacted, the teacher then calls "Red Flag." Together the teacher and the student evaluate his response and record this on the Red Flag homework sheet. See Figure 12 (p. 90) for an example of a completed Red Flag assignment, and a blank form in Figure 13 (p. 91).

It is very important that the student initially be given advance warning that a Red Flag approach will be used (i.e., telling him exactly when he will be "set up"), as the goal of this assignment is for the student to perform the skill behaviors successfully. If the teacher, for example, suddenly and without warning, begins to berate a child to see how he will deal with this situation, serious damage may be done to the student–teacher relationship. As the student becomes more familiar with this process, less advance notice can be given. This technique, similar to Meichenbaum and Cameron's (1983) Stress Inoculation Training, emphasizes the importance of the student's being able to perform the skill under stressful conditions.

One additional caution must be mentioned. When imple-

Figure 10. Homework 1 Report

Student: _Brian_   Date: _Sept. 9_

Skill: _Asking a Favor_

Steps:
1. Decide if you want or need to ask a favor.
2. Plan what you want to say.
3. Ask the favor in a friendly way.
4. Remember to thank the person.

Who will I try this with? _Bill and Michelle_

When? _reading group_

What happened? _I asked them to move. They moved_

How did I do?

Why did I circle this? _I didn't say thank you._

Figure 11. Blank Homework 1 Report

Student:_____ Date:_____

Skill:_____

Steps:

Who will I try this with?_____

When?_____

What happened?_____

_____

_____

How did I do?

Why did I circle this?_____

_____

Figure 12. Red Flag (Homework 2) Report

Student: __Todd_____ Date: __October 20__

Skill: __Asking for help_____

Steps: 1. Ask myself "Can I do this alone?

2. Raise my hand

3. Wait, I know I can wait without talking

4. Ask in a friendly way

How did I do?

Why did I circle this? __I did all the steps.__

Figure 13. Blank Red Flag (Homework 2) Report

Student: _____   Date: _____

Skill: _____

Steps:

_____

How did I do?

Why did I circle this? _____

_____

menting the Red Flag technique, the teacher or other group leader should be the only person creating the simulated stressful situation. Other students should not be instructed to tease another student, for example. They should not be placed in the position of having to behave in inappropriate ways, even for the sake of making a situation appear more realistic. Therefore, this stage of homework does not lend itself easily to use with skills such as Dealing with Group Pressure and can be omitted for skills such as these.

Homework 3 (Skillstreaming—Self-Recording). The child who has almost achieved the mastery level of a particular skill (i.e., who knows the steps well and shows success with the other stages of homework) is ready to attempt self-recording or monitoring her own skill use. The student completes the relevant information on the Skillstreaming—Self-Recording homework sheet, including the behavioral skill steps for the target skill. Then, throughout the course of the day, the student lists when the steps of the skill were practiced and completes the self-evaluation portion of the homework sheet according to the same criteria used in other homework assignments. For special education students this can be a useful technique to increase the chances that they will practice a given skill in non-special education settings, such as mainstream classrooms, if appropriate, or at home or in the community. This homework assignment may assist in the transfer of learning to the setting to which the student is slated eventually to return. An example of a completed Skillstreaming—Self-Recording homework assignment is presented in Figure 14. Figure 15 is a blank form.

Homework 4. In this stage of homework, more than one skill is listed on a 3 × 5-inch index card. The student then tallies each time he practices the skill throughout the school day, in his neighborhood, and at home. This method of self-recording gives the older student an inconspicuous way to chart skills used outside of his classroom (e.g., on the playground, in the school cafeteria). Figure 16 presents a completed example of this stage of homework.

Use of Homework Reports. The first part of each Structured Learning session is devoted to presenting and discussing homework reports. When students have made an effort to complete

Figure 14. Skillstreaming—Self-Recording (Homework 3) Report

Student: *Michelle*   Date: *Sept. 30*

Skill: *Staying Out of Fights*

Steps:
1. Stop and count to 10.
2. Decide what the problem is.
3. Think of other ways to deal with the problem.
   a. walk away for now.
   b. talk to the person in a friendly way?
   c. ask someone for help.
4. Act out your best choice.

When I Practiced   How did I do?

on the bus

morning recess

music

after school

Figure 15. Blank Skillstreaming—Self-Recording (Homework 3) Report

Student:_____ Date:_____

Skill: _____

Steps:

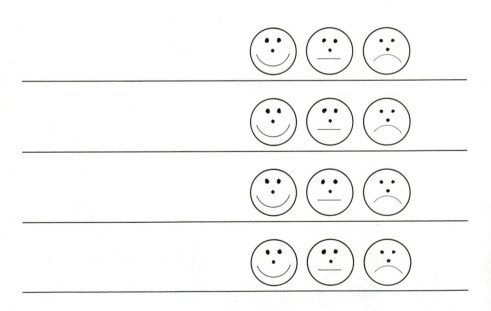

When I Practiced   How did I do?

Figure 16. Homework 4 Index Card

```
┌─────────────────────────────────────────────┐
│                                               │
│      Brian              Nov. 28-30            │
│   Asking a Favor            |||               │
│   Making a Complaint          |               │
│                                               │
│                                               │
└─────────────────────────────────────────────┘
```

their homework assignments, the group leaders should provide social reinforcement, while failure to do homework should be met with some chagrin and expressed disappointment. It cannot be stressed too strongly that without attempts such as these to maximize transfer, the value of the entire teaching effort is in severe jeopardy.

The majority of elementary school children will be able to successfully progress through all four stages of homework assignments. If, however, particular students, such as first- or second-grade children or young handicapped children, are unsuccessful with the more independent levels of homework (Stages 3 and 4), these may be simplified or eliminated to suit the skill level of the child. For example, instead of requesting that a first-grade child complete Homework 3 (self-recording) as presented, the child may be asked to inform his teacher immediately after he has used a skill in the school setting; the teacher may then place a sticker or a star on a chart to record the student's performance of this skill.

Group Self-Report Chart.   Group self-recording is a valuable additional component of the homework process, which some schools have employed by use of the Group Self-Report Chart (see Figure 17). In this method, the teacher asks each child to state which skills he has used during the day in various real-life settings, and then asks him to make a tally mark under his name on the chart, next to the skill he practiced. For very young elementary school children, stickers or stars may be

Figure 17. Group Self-Report Chart

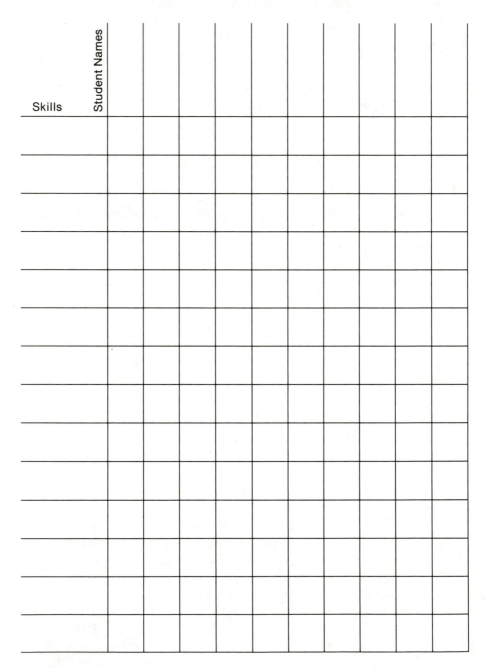

used instead of tally marks. Time should be allowed for this in the school day schedule, usually 10 minutes at the end of the day. Both the teacher and the student's peers should provide reinforcement to him for the practice of these prosocial skills. As time permits, several students should be asked to cite the specific situations in which a skill was performed and the students, again, should receive praise for these self-reports. While the primary purpose of this chart is to enhance the students' use of prosocial skills, there is an added benefit of this technique. The Group Self-Report Chart provides a record of the skills the students actually are practicing and gives the teacher an indication of the specific skills that are not being used frequently. He will then know which skills need to be reviewed or taught again.

SUMMARY OF TEACHER PROCEDURES FOR CONDUCTING A STRUCTURED LEARNING SESSION

The material in this chapter provides most of what the typical Structured Learning group leader will need to know in order to lead skill-enhancing Structured Learning groups. To assist further, we have provided an outline of procedures for conducting an initial Structured Learning session as well as for the subsequent sessions.

INITIAL STRUCTURED LEARNING SESSION

A. Review the group rules or "Helpful Reminders" formulated in the Preparation Session (see Chapter 4).
Example: —"What is one reminder that we decided on?" (Refer to the chart of Helpful Reminders.)
B. Review the reinforcement plan described in the Preparation Session (see Chapter 4).
Examples:—"What do you receive tokens for?" (following the group rules, participating, practicing the skills)
—"What do you do with the tokens you earn?"
—"What do you trade them in for?"
—"When can you trade them?"
C. Compile a list of prosocial skills that the students feel they need to learn. Use the list generated from teacher and student suggestions in the Preparation Session (see Chapter 4) as a starting point.

    Examples:—"What were some of the social skills we discussed
                last time?"
                —"Here is the list of social skills we came up with.
                Let's read the list together."

D. Review the procedures for learning the skills.
    Examples:—Show (modeling): "First we'll show you the way to
                do it."
                —Try (role play): "Then you'll try it."
                —Discuss (feedback): "Then we'll talk about how you
                did."
                —Practice (transfer): "Then you'll try it on your own."

E. Introduce the idea of breaking a skill down into steps to make it
   easier.
    Examples:—"What are the steps in learning to play basketball
                (or volleyball, checkers, or any game of interest)?"
                —"What do you do first? Second?" (etc.)
                —"What are the steps or things you must do to show
                someone that you are listening?" (Ask for the spe-
                cific behaviors.)

F. Proceed to the first skill, following the outline that will be used
   for all succeeding sessions.

SUBSEQUENT STRUCTURED LEARNING SESSIONS

A. Have students report homework assignments on their assigned
   skill.
    Examples:—"Who has a homework report today?"
                —"Michelle, will you tell us how your homework
                assignment went?"
    (Provide reinforcement for the assignments that were completed.)
                —"Were you happy with the way you performed the
                skill?"
                —"Were you happy with the way things turned out?"
                —"Would you do anything differently next time?"

B. Present an overview of the skill to be worked on in this session.
   Ask questions that will help the students define the skill in their
   own language.
    Examples:—"Who can tell me what _____ is?"
                —"What does _____ mean?"

C. Formulate the skill steps.
    Examples:—"We're going to talk about the steps or parts of
                knowing your own feelings."
                —"How do you know that you are having a strong
                feeling?"
                —"How does your body feel?"

—"What do you need to decide next?"

(List the steps to the skill on the chalkboard or on a chart, using the steps in Chapter 6 as a guide.)

D. Present the modeling displays.
1. Ask the students to follow each step in the modeling display as it is depicted.
2. Present two relevant examples of using the skill, following its behavioral steps.

(Since a group may spend several sessions on the same skill, we recommend that each exposure to a skill include at least two new modeling vignettes.)

E. Discuss the modeling of the skill.
1. Discuss the way the modeling may remind students of situations involving skill usage in their own lives.

Example: —"Did any of the situations you just saw remind you of times you have had to _____?"

2. Ask questions that encourage the students to talk about times when they have needed or might need to use the skill.

Examples: —"What do you do in situations where you have to _____?"

—"Have you ever had to _____?"

F. Organize the role play.
1. Ask a student who has volunteered a situation to tell more about how the skill could be used in a similar situation—where, when, and with whom the skill might be useful in the future.
2. Designate this student as a main actor, and ask him to choose a co-actor (someone who reminds him most of the person with whom the skill will be used in the real-life situation).

Examples: —"What does _____ look like?"

—"Who in the group reminds you of _____ in some way?"

3. Get additional information from the main actor, if necessary, and set the stage for the role playing (including props and furniture arrangement).

Examples: —"Where might you be talking to _____?"

—"How is it furnished?"

—"Would you be standing or sitting?"

4. Rehearse with the main actor what he will say and do during the role play.

Example: —"What will you say for Step 1 of the skill?"

5. Just prior to the role playing, give each group member some final instructions as to his part.

Examples:—To the main actor: "Try to follow the steps as best you can."

　　　　—To the co-actor: "Try to play the part of ＿＿＿＿ as
　　　　best you can. Say and do what you think ＿＿＿＿
　　　　would do."

　　　　—To the other students in the group: "Watch how
　　　　well ＿＿＿＿ follows the steps so that we can talk
　　　　about it after the role play." Or "＿＿＿＿, will you
　　　　watch to see if ＿＿＿＿ follows Step 1; ＿＿＿＿, will
　　　　you watch to see if he follows Step 2"; and so on.

G.　Instruct the role players to begin.

　　1.　One group leader should be positioned near the actors to
　　　　provide whatever coaching or prompting is needed by the
　　　　actor or co-actor.

　　2.　The other group leader should sit with the observing students
　　　　and help them pay attention to the role play.

　　3.　In the event that the role play strays markedly from the
　　　　behavioral steps, the leader should stop the scene, provide
　　　　needed instruction, and begin again.

H.　Provide feedback following the role play.

　　1.　Ask the main actor to wait until he has heard everyone's
　　　　comments before evaluating his own performance.

　　2.　Ask the co-actor "In the role of ＿＿＿＿, how did ＿＿＿＿
　　　　make you feel?"

　　3.　Ask the observers "Did ＿＿＿＿ follow Step 1? How do you
　　　　know?" (Have them specify the main actor's behaviors.) Con-
　　　　tinue for all the steps.

　　Examples:—"What specific things did you like or dislike?"
　　　　　　　—"In what ways did the co-actor do a good job?"

　　4.　Comment on the way the main actor followed the behavioral
　　　　steps; provide praise and/or tokens; point out what was done
　　　　well; and comment on what else might be done to make the
　　　　enactment even better.

　　5.　Ask the main actor: "How do you feel you did?" "How do you
　　　　think the steps worked out?"

I.　Help the main role player to plan homework.

　　1.　Ask the main actor when, where, and with whom he might
　　　　attempt the skill before the next class meeting.

　　2.　Choose the appropriate stage of homework and explain it to
　　　　the student. (Assist each student in filling in his homework
　　　　sheet at the end of the group session.)

　　3.　Students who have not had a chance to role play during the
　　　　session may be assigned homework in the form of looking
　　　　for situations relevant to the skill that they might role play
　　　　during the next Structured Learning session. They should be
　　　　cautioned *not* to attempt the skill outside the group until
　　　　they have role played it in the group.

SUMMARY

This chapter described the procedural information necessary to begin effective Structured Learning groups. The sequence of Structured Learning components and step-by-step procedures for conducting the initial Structured Learning session and subsequent Structured Learning sessions have been examined. The following chapter provides the specific prosocial skills to be taught, along with recommended behavioral steps to achieve successful performance of each skill.

CHAPTER 6

Prosocial Skills

This chapter presents the Structured Learning curriculum, a diverse series of prosocial skills and their behavioral steps, designed to assist the elementary-age skill-deficient child in achieving skill competency. The 60 prosocial skills that follow are divided into the following five skill groups: (1) Classroom Survival Skills; (2) Friendship-Making Skills; (3) Skills for Dealing with Feelings; (4) Skill Alternatives to Aggression; and (5) Skills for Dealing with Stress. The skills presented are those believed to be related to a child's social competence (Spivak & Shure, 1974); those suggested by research to be related to peer acceptance (Mesibov & LaGreca, 1981), positive teacher attention, and academic success (Cartledge & Milburn, 1980); and those likely to provide effective performance and personal satisfaction in the student's natural environment (Goldstein, Sprafkin, Gershaw, & Klein, 1980). This skill curriculum is by no means all-inclusive. As students express concerns and difficulties they are experiencing, and as the teacher observes problems the students encounter, new skills can and should be developed for instruction. Furthermore, in individual instances —depending on the child and her real-life circumstances—it may be appropriate to retain and teach a given skill but alter one or more of its behavioral steps. It will often be the case that both teacher and student together will effectively engage in this skill development or skill alteration process.

SELECTION OF SKILLS

In selecting the skills for instruction, primary emphasis should be placed on meeting the students' personal development and social needs as perceived by the students themselves. Teaching those skills that will provide students with positive alternatives for dealing with their immediate needs will serve to increase their feelings of social competence, as well as their desire to learn other relevant skills. When students perceive a need to learn a new behavior, and then have the opportunity to use that newly acquired behavior in situations that will benefit them, learning is likely to be far more effective and enduring.

Selecting skills that are important to others in the students' environment, such as parents and teachers, should also be considered. For example, parents can convey information about the specific skills needed in children's home and neighborhood settings. The teacher can then discuss such skills with the Structured Learning group to discover which seem most relevant to them, and order the teaching of the skills accordingly. A second possible benefit of such parental consultation is pinpointing a skill that may be useful in the school setting but which may be contradictory to the expectations of home and neighborhood. Information from the parents is therefore needed to guide the teacher in emphasizing to the participating students the specific environments in which a particular skill can be most useful to them. Instruction in prosocial skills valued by the children's parents, teachers, and peers also increases the likelihood that positive reinforcement will be given to them when performing these skills in natural, real-life environments. Such reinforcement may assist in maintaining the use of the prosocial skill once the actual teaching in the Structured Learning group ceases (Stokes & Baer, 1977).

The majority of the behavioral skill steps outlined in this chapter are oriented to children in grades three and four. It may be necessary to modify certain skill steps to meet the needs of certain groups of students. For example, steps may appropriately be made more complex for the older child, as shown in the following example.

Skill 3: Saying Thank You

1. Decide if you want to thank someone.
2. Decide how you want to thank them.
   a. Say thank you for _____.
   b. Say how you feel about what they did.
   c. Do something nice for that person.
3. Choose a good time and place.
4. Act out your best choice.

Students in the upper elementary grades will guide the leaders of Structured Learning groups to the level of complexity in these steps that they are able to handle.

It will also often be necessary to simplify many behavioral skill steps for effective instruction of children in the primary grades. Pictoral cues that illustrate these steps will further clarify the steps for such younger children and other non-readers. Some examples of such simplifications are presented in Figure 18. In addition to simplifying the wording of skill steps, and providing pictoral cues to accompany them, it will often prove helpful with younger students to simplify the names of the skills to be taught. Examples include:

Skill 6: Completing Assignments—change to Finishing Work

Skill 11: Making Corrections—change to Fixing Mistakes

Skill 25: Apologizing—change to Saying Sorry

Skill 27: Expressing Your Feelings—change to Saying What You Feel

Skill 30: Expressing Concern for Another—change to Caring

Skill 32: Dealing with Another's Anger—change to When Someone Is Angry with You

There will be children for whom Structured Learning participation is too difficult even after such simplification. For some of these children, the difficulty may be not the language of the skill training sequence, but a failure of or deficiency in those abilities necessary for satisfactory group task functioning (e.g., the ability to sit at a desk, the ability to stay on task for a short period of time, the ability to understand directions). Deficiencies in such prerequisite competencies will have to be remediated by teacher efforts, maturation, or other means

Figure 18. Simplifications of Skill Steps for Young Children

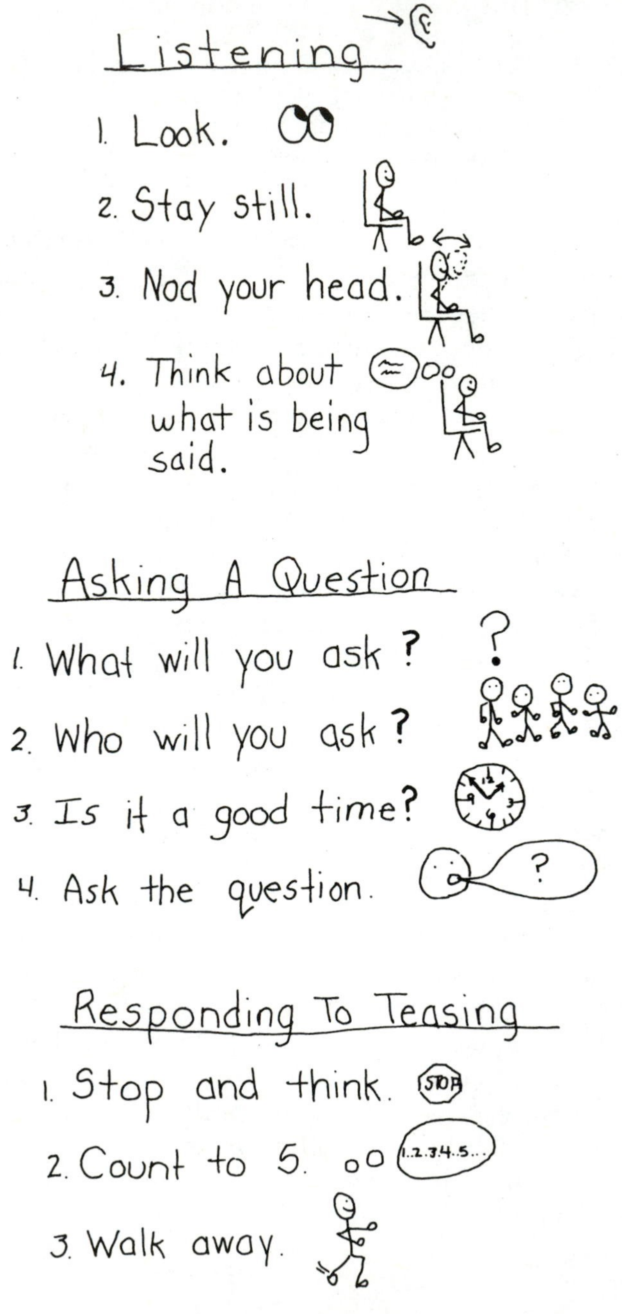
Listening
1. Look.
2. Stay still.
3. Nod your head.
4. Think about what is being said.
Asking A Question
1. What will you ask?
2. Who will you ask?
3. Is it a good time?
4. Ask the question.
?
Responding To Teasing
1. Stop and think.
STOP
2. Count to 5.
1..2..3..4..5...
3. Walk away.

prior to the inclusion of such students in the Structured Learning teaching process.

SEQUENCE OF SKILLS

It is not necessary that the skills presented in this chapter be taught in the sequence in which they are listed. We have found, however, that the first several skills of Group I (Classroom Survival Skills) and Group II (Friendship-Making Skills) are excellent skills to orient both students and leaders to Structured Learning. As noted before, once the students become familiar with Structured Learning, the skills chosen for teaching should be those that are relevant to the immediate needs of the students. For example, a child who experiences anxiety and frustration at being teased by her peers will be far more motivated to learn the skill of Responding to Teasing than one of the Classroom Survival Skills.

BEHAVIORAL STEPS

Each skill is task-analyzed into specific behavioral steps that will guide the student in successful performance of the skill. The first step of many of the skills, specifically those dealing with alternatives to aggression, provides students with an impulse-control strategy. Before students can break their well-established pattern of skill-deficient responding and perform a prosocial alternative, their initial reaction to the conflict situation must be stopped. Therefore, the student needs to learn strategies such as counting to five or taking three deep breaths for use when the problem first arises. This will give the students needed time to recall the remainder of the behavioral steps.

As noted previously, behavioral steps can and should be adjusted to meet the needs of unique situations and particular student groups. For example, specific classroom rules can be incorporated into the steps of the Classroom Survival Skills. As a classroom or special education teacher, if you normally request that a student ask a peer for assistance with an academic task, for instance, then this should be incorporated as a behavioral step into the appropriate prosocial skill. Additionally, allowing the students themselves to assist in selecting and framing particular steps, and rephrasing the steps in language more easily understood by them, will further their commitment and ability to master these steps.

Each skill and the behavioral steps to successfully enacting that skill are presented next. Skills marked by an asterisk in the following list are ones suggested for beginning Structured Learning instruction. Suggestions for enhancing the effectiveness of skill training, suggested situations for modeling displays, and additional skill-usage comments are also provided.

Two general comments on using these skills should be made here. First, it should be remembered that when skill steps are modeled or role played, the main actor should "think aloud" those skill steps that are normally thought to oneself so that students can observe the cognitive processes related to acting appropriately. Second, the items under Notes for Discussion or Comments that suggest having students draw up personal lists of activities, such as ones to fill up free time, are written with the assumption that students will save these lists in their individual prosocial skills folders, which they may keep at the end of training (see Skill 45 Comments, and Chapter 8, p. 185).

<h2 style="text-align:center">Prosocial Skills</h2>

Group I. Classroom Survival Skills
*1. Listening
*2. Asking for Help
*3. Saying Thank You
*4. Bringing Materials to Class
 5. Following Instructions
 6. Completing Assignments
 7. Contributing to Discussions
 8. Offering Help to an Adult
 9. Asking a Question
10. Ignoring Distractions
11. Making Corrections
12. Deciding on Something to Do
13. Setting a Goal

Group II. Friendship-Making Skills
*14. Introducing Yourself
*15. Beginning a Conversation
*16. Ending a Conversation
*17. Joining In
*18. Playing a Game

*19. Asking a Favor
*20. Offering Help to a Classmate
 21. Giving a Compliment
 22. Accepting a Compliment
 23. Suggesting an Activity
 24. Sharing
 25. Apologizing

Group III. Skills for Dealing with Feelings

 26. Knowing Your Feelings
 27. Expressing Your Feelings
 28. Recognizing Another's Feelings
 29. Showing Understanding of Another's Feelings
 30. Expressing Concern for Another
 31. Dealing with Your Anger
 32. Dealing with Another's Anger
 33. Expressing Affection
 34. Dealing with Fear
 35. Rewarding Yourself

Group IV. Skill Alternatives to Aggression

 36. Using Self-control
 37. Asking Permission
 38. Responding to Teasing
 39. Avoiding Trouble
 40. Staying Out of Fights
 41. Problem Solving
 42. Accepting Consequences
 43. Dealing with an Accusation
 44. Negotiating

Group V. Skills for Dealing with Stress

 45. Dealing with Boredom
 46. Deciding What Caused a Problem
 47. Making a Complaint
 48. Answering a Complaint
 49. Dealing with Losing
 50. Showing Sportsmanship
 51. Dealing with Being Left Out
 52. Dealing with Embarrassment
 53. Reacting to Failure
 54. Accepting No
 55. Saying No
 56. Relaxing
 57. Dealing with Group Pressure
 58. Dealing with Wanting Something That Isn't Mine
 59. Making a Decision
 60. Being Honest

GROUP I: CLASSROOM SURVIVAL SKILLS
Skill 1: Listening

STEPS	NOTES FOR DISCUSSION
1. Look at the person who is talking.	Point out to students that sometimes others may think someone isn't listening, even though he/she really is. These steps are to *show* someone that you are really listening.
2. Remember to sit quietly.	Tell students to face the person and remember not to laugh, fidget, play with something, etc.
3. Think about what is being said.	
4. Say yes or nod your head.	
5. Ask a question about the topic to find out more.	Discuss relevant questions (i.e., ones that do not change the topic).

SUGGESTED SITUATIONS

School: Your teacher explains an assignment.

Home: Your parents are talking with you about a problem.

Peer group: Another student tells of a T.V. program he/she watched or what he/she did over the weekend.

COMMENTS

This is an excellent skill with which to begin your Structured Learning group. Once the skill of Listening is learned by students, it is useful to incorporate it into group or classroom rules.

It is important to emphasize *showing* someone the behaviors that indicate that the student is listening. When a student is talking with the teacher, it is useful for the teacher to model these listening behaviors.

GROUP I: CLASSROOM SURVIVAL SKILLS
Skill 2: Asking for Help

STEPS	NOTES FOR DISCUSSION
1. Ask yourself "Can I do this alone?"	Students should be sure to read directions and try the assignment on their own (at least one problem or question).
2. If not, raise your hand.	Discuss that this is appropriate in class, not at home or with friends.
3. Wait. Say to yourself "I know I can wait without talking."	Instruct the students to say this to themselves until the desired help is given.
4. Ask for help in a friendly way.	Discuss what constitutes a friendly manner (e.g., tone of voice, facial expression, content).

SUGGESTED SITUATIONS

School: You want help with an assignment, or you don't understand what you are supposed to do.

Home: You can't find your skates and ask your mom to help look for them.

Peer group: You want your friend to teach you a new dance that everyone is doing at birthday parties.

COMMENTS

It is very important to discuss body language, or "body talk," with the students throughout Structured Learning. When first introducing terminology such as "in a friendly way," spending time discussing and modeling friendly behaviors and nonverbal communicators is essential.

GROUP I: CLASSROOM SURVIVAL SKILLS
Skill 3: Saying Thank You

STEPS	NOTES FOR DISCUSSION
1. Decide if you want to thank someone.	Discuss the purpose of saying thank you (i.e., it's a way of telling someone that you appreciate what he/she did). Emphasize that this must be sincere. You thank someone when you want to or feel it is deserved, such as for a favor, help given, or a compliment.
2. Choose a good time and place.	Discuss how to choose a good time: when the person is not busy with something or someone else.
3. Thank the person in a friendly way.	Let students know that it is okay to tell why you are thanking the person (i.e., that they really needed the help or that something the person did made them feel good).

SUGGESTED SITUATIONS

School: Someone helps you with your schoolwork.

Home: Your parents help you with your chores or your homework, or let you do something you have asked to do.

Peer group: Someone lends you a pencil, or compliments you.

COMMENTS

The use of this skill may appear very mechanical in the beginning. The students may also begin to use this skill frequently following initial instruction. This is quite natural, and should not be interpreted as insincere use of the skill.

It may be useful to discuss and practice different ways of saying thank you (e.g., "It made me feel good when you . . ."; doing something nice for the person).

GROUP I: CLASSROOM SURVIVAL SKILLS
SKILL 4: **Bringing Materials to Class**

STEPS	NOTES FOR DISCUSSION
1. Ask yourself "What materials do I need for this class?"	Students may have to make a list of needed items, such as a pencil, crayons, paper, or notebook.
2. Gather the materials together.	Students should remember not to take something that isn't needed (e.g., toys).
3. Ask yourself "Do I have everything I need?"	
4. Recheck your materials and pack them up.	

SUGGESTED SITUATIONS

School: You are going to a special area class (e.g., art, music, physical education), or attending a class in another classroom.

Home: You are going to attend outside club events or activities (e.g., Boy Scouts, Girl Scouts, church activities).

Peer group: You will be staying overnight at a friend's house.

COMMENTS

This skill assists the students in becoming more organized. For some students, providing a written list of what is needed may be necessary initially. Also, providing a notebook or folder where the materials can be kept may assist students in performing this skill.

Posting a "cue card" (the list of the skill steps) near the doorway or on the classroom door may help students to remember to check for the materials they will need before they leave the classroom.

GROUP I: CLASSROOM SURVIVAL SKILLS
Skill 5: Following Instructions

STEPS	NOTES FOR DISCUSSION
1. Listen carefully to the instructions.	Remind students that they should think about what is being said.
2. Ask questions about anything you don't understand.	Students should be taught the skill Asking for Help (Skill 2) or Asking a Question (Skill 9).
3. Repeat the instructions to the person (or to yourself).	This step is necessary to be sure that the directions are clearly understood.
4. Follow the instructions.	

SUGGESTED SITUATIONS

School: A teacher explains an assignment.

Home: Your mom or dad gives you instructions on how to cook.

Peer group: A friend gives you directions for getting to his/her house.

COMMENTS

It is crucial that the students be able to complete the task requested of them independently. The skill will only serve to frustrate students if they follow the steps to Following Instructions and then find the task is far too difficult for them.

GROUP I: CLASSROOM SURVIVAL SKILLS
SKILL 6: Completing Assignments

STEPS	NOTES FOR DISCUSSION
1. Ask yourself "Is my work finished?"	Have students practice reviewing each item to be certain that all questions are answered.
2. Look over each question to be sure.	Remind students to fill in the missing answers if items aren't complete.
3. When you are sure your work is finished, hand it in.	Specific classroom rules for handing in completed work can be included in this step.
4. Say to yourself "Good for me! I finished it!"	Discuss ways of rewarding oneself.

SUGGESTED SITUATIONS

School: Complete academic assignments given by the teacher or activities at a learning center.

Home: Finish a project or activity you started at home (making a toy spaceship from a kit or cleaning your room).

Peer group: Complete a project you promised to do for a friend.

COMMENTS

This skill facilitates organizational ability and is particularly useful for the learning disabled student or others who have specific difficulties in task completion.

It should be noted that this skill ideally should be practiced in the setting where the skill is needed. For example, if practice in seatwork completion is needed, the students should practice this skill at their desks.

Again, it is most important that students have the skills, knowledge, and motor responses needed to successfully complete the assignment. Therefore, the teacher must be certain that the task requested is one students can, in fact, complete independently.

Self-reward (Step 4) is a skill (Skill 35) that may provide the student with necessary reinforcement until the skill can be reinforced by the teacher or parent.

GROUP I: CLASSROOM SURVIVAL SKILLS
Skill 7: Contributing to Discussions

STEPS	NOTES FOR DISCUSSION
1. Decide if you have something you want to say.	
2. Ask yourself "Is this related to the discussion?"	Discuss that the comments must be relevant to the discussion. Give examples of relevant comments.
3. Decide exactly what you want to say.	Students may need the additional step of deciding how to say it.
4. Raise your hand.	Steps 4 and 5 should be in accordance with your classroom rules. Students should be told to eliminate these steps for use at home and with friends.
5. When you are called on, say what you want to say.	

SUGGESTED SITUATIONS

School: Say something in a class discussion when you have something you want to say.

Home: Say something in a family meeting or during dinner.

Peer group: Say something in a discussion with friends after school.

COMMENTS

Emphasis can be placed on when this skill is appropriate to use. For example, some teachers may not want a class discussion of a particular topic. The students must learn the cues communicated by a given teacher that indicate that contributing is not acceptable.

Additionally, the students should be able to discriminate among the persons with whom the skill is used. For example, contributing to a discussion among friends would be carried out differently in manner and content than contributing to a discussion in class.

When providing the opportunities to practice this skill, the teacher should choose topics for discussion that the students have knowledge of and an interest in.

GROUP I: CLASSROOM SURVIVAL SKILLS
Skill 8: Offering Help to an Adult

STEPS	NOTES FOR DISCUSSION
1. Decide if the adult needs your help.	Discuss how the student can tell if the adult could use the help.
2. Think of what you may do to help.	
3. Decide how to ask if you can help.	Discuss different ways of asking (e.g., "May I help you do that?").
4. Ask yourself "Is this a good time to offer help?"	Remind students to be sure that their work is completed and there isn't something else they are supposed to do. If this is not a good time, they should wait until it is a good time.
5. Ask the adult if you may help.	
6. Help the adult.	Discuss the importance of following through with help.

SUGGESTED SITUATIONS

School: The teacher is making a bulletin board or rearranging the classroom.

Home: Your mom or dad is fixing dinner.

COMMENTS

With some students, it is especially important to emphasize the step of deciding if the teacher or parent needs the help (Step 1). A student who frequently requests to help may be using this as a method of gaining attention or a way to avoid academic tasks. However, in such cases this skill can be useful to teach the student when it is appropriate to offer assistance.

GROUP I: CLASSROOM SURVIVAL SKILLS
Skill 9: Asking a Question

STEPS	NOTES FOR DISCUSSION
1. Decide what you need to ask.	Discuss how students can decide whether they really need to ask this question.
2. Decide whom you will ask.	Discuss how to decide whether to ask the teacher, an aide, a classmate, or someone else.
3. Decide how you will ask.	Stress asking in a friendly way: that it is not only what is said, but how it is said (e.g., you will have a better chance of getting an answer if you ask with a friendly look and tone of voice).
4. Choose a good time and place.	Discuss how to choose a good time (when the other person isn't busy or talking with someone) and when to follow classroom rules.
5. Ask your question.	
6. Thank the person for giving you the answer.	Students should be taught the skill Saying Thank You (Skill 3).

SUGGESTED SITUATIONS

School: Ask the teacher about something you don't understand.

Home: Ask your mom and dad about their work or hobbies.

Peer group: Ask another student how to play a game.

COMMENTS

It will be appropriate to discuss the times when asking a question is needed. Students should be encouraged to use this skill only when a legitimate question needs to be asked. The discussion, therefore, can include other ways of finding needed information (e.g., consulting a dictionary or encyclopedia).

GROUP I: CLASSROOM SURVIVAL SKILLS
SKILL 10: Ignoring Distractions

STEPS	NOTES FOR DISCUSSION
1. Count to five.	Discuss that counting to five will give the student the time needed to recall the remainder of the steps to the skill.
2. Say to yourself "I won't look. I'll keep on working."	These statements should be spoken out loud during modeling and role playing.
3. Continue to work.	
4. Say to yourself "Good for me. I did it!"	Discuss ways of rewarding oneself.

SUGGESTED SITUATIONS

School: Another teacher comes into the room to talk with your teacher.

Home: Your brother or sister tries to distract you from your chores or homework.

Peer group: A classmate tries to get your attention in class or to distract you from a game at recess.

COMMENTS

It may help if the student gives himself/herself a check mark on a card for each time he/she ignores a distraction. This self-recording card can then be shown to the teacher for additional praise or other reinforcement if needed.

Self-reward (Step 4) is a skill (Skill 35) that may provide the student with necessary reinforcement until the skill can be reinforced by the teacher or parent.

GROUP I: CLASSROOM SURVIVAL SKILLS
SKILL 11: Making Corrections

STEPS	NOTES FOR DISCUSSION
1. Look at the first correction.	Discuss dealing with one correction at a time, rather than looking at them all. This will help lessen the frustration of having to do a task over again.
2. Try to answer the question (or do the task) again.	
3. If you don't understand the question, ask someone.	Students should be taught the skill Asking for Help (Skill 2).
4. Write in your new answer (or do the activity over).	Discuss the feeling of frustration when tasks must be done again.
5. Say to yourself "Good. That one is done."	
6. Go on to the next correction.	

SUGGESTED SITUATIONS

School: A math assignment is given back to you to correct.

Home: You must do a chore over again.

Peer group: You made something for a friend, but it didn't turn out right.

COMMENTS

Redoing tasks or academic assignments can be extremely frustrating for young children. This skill should assist with dealing with this type of frustration. It is crucial that the task be within the skills of the student. If many errors are made on any assignment, it is most important that the teacher analyze these errors and reteach the necessary skills. The skill of Making Corrections is most useful following such a reteaching effort or for assignments that are completed carelessly.

GROUP I: CLASSROOM SURVIVAL SKILLS
Skill 12: Deciding on Something to Do

STEPS	NOTES FOR DISCUSSION
1. Check to be sure you have finished all of your work.	For many young students, an assignment sheet where the student can check off work as it is completed will assist with this first step.
2. Think of the activities you would like to do.	Generate a list of acceptable activities. Students should be sure these activities are within the rules.
3. Choose one.	Students should be sure the activity chosen will not disrupt classmates who have not yet completed their schoolwork (or brothers or sisters, if the students are at home).
4. Start the activity.	

SUGGESTED SITUATIONS

School: Decide on an activity during free time in the classroom or when you have a few minutes after finishing your work.

Home: Choose something to do after you have finished your homework and chores.

COMMENTS

It would be helpful if the students generated a list of quiet activities (those in which they could engage when other students are still working on their academic tasks) and less quiet ones (those activities in which they can participate during a free activity period for the entire class). These, along with the behavioral steps needed to achieve the skill, could then be displayed in the classroom for easy student reference.

Dealing with Boredom (Skill 45) is a similar skill geared for use outside of the academic learning setting.

GROUP I: CLASSROOM SURVIVAL SKILLS
Skill 13: Setting a Goal

STEPS	NOTES FOR DISCUSSION
1. Decide on a goal you want to reach.	Discuss choosing a realistic goal (i.e., content, time frame).
2. Decide on the steps you will need to take to get there.	It may be helpful to list the steps and post the list on a bulletin board or include it in a student folder.
3. Take the first step.	
4. Take all other steps, one at a time.	Have the students mark off each step as it is achieved or place a sticker on the list of steps.
5. Reward yourself when your goal is reached.	Discuss ways of rewarding oneself.

SUGGESTED SITUATIONS

School: Set and reach an academic goal.

Home: Clean your room or the garage.

Peer group: Make a new friend.

COMMENTS

Many elementary-age students enjoy setting academic goals (e.g., learning addition facts, reading a given number of books). It is important that these goals be within their reach within a relatively short period of time. Setting small goals that can be easily achieved (e.g., learning the addition facts to sums of 10) is more beneficial than setting goals that will take students a long time.

Goal setting is also useful for nonacademic areas, such as prosocial skills development. Examples of such goals might include practicing a given skill a certain number of times or using it in home or peer group settings.

Self-reward (Step 5) is a skill (Skill 35) that may provide the student with necessary reinforcement until the skill can be reinforced by the teacher or parent.

GROUP II: FRIENDSHIP-MAKING SKILLS
Skill 14: Introducing Yourself

STEPS	NOTES FOR DISCUSSION
1. Decide if you want to meet the person.	Discuss why students might want to meet a person: the person looks friendly, the person is new to the school, etc.
2. Decide if it is a good time.	Discuss how to choose a good time: when the person is not busy with something or someone else.
3. Walk up to the person.	Watch for appropriate distance.
4. Introduce yourself.	Discuss ways to introduce yourself (e.g., say "Hi, my name is _____").
5. Wait for the person to tell you his/her name. If he/she doesn't tell you, ask.	Discuss appropriate ways to ask a person's name.

SUGGESTED SITUATIONS

School: There is a new student in your classroom.

Home: A friend of your parents is visiting your home.

Peer group: A new boy or girl moves into your neighborhood.

COMMENTS

Practicing this skill will also assist a child in knowing what to do when someone introduces himself/herself.
    When this skill is learned have the students go on to the skill of Beginning a Conversation (Skill 15).

GROUP II: FRIENDSHIP-MAKING SKILLS
Skill 15: Beginning a Conversation

STEPS	NOTES FOR DISCUSSION
1. Choose whom you want to talk with.	Remind students to consider whether their talking is going to bother someone else, for example, someone who is trying to work.
2. Decide what you want to say.	Suggest as topics something the students did during the weekend or something that is bothering them.
3. Choose a good time and place.	Discuss how to choose a good time: when the other person isn't busy or when the student isn't supposed to be doing something else.
4. Start talking in a friendly way.	Discuss the body language and nonverbal communicators that show a friendly attitude, and suggest watching the person to see if he/she seems interested and not talking too long without giving the other person a chance to talk.

SUGGESTED SITUATIONS

School: Tell a classmate about an art project you did.

Home: Tell your parents what happened at school.

Peer group: Tell a friend what you did during the weekend.

COMMENTS

It is recommended that this skill be taught directly following Skill 14 (Introducing Yourself). Skill 16 (Ending a Conversation) is suggested as a follow-up skill.

GROUP II: FRIENDSHIP-MAKING SKILLS
Skill 16: Ending a Conversation

STEPS	NOTES FOR DISCUSSION
1. Decide if you need to finish the conversation.	
2. Decide the reason you need to end the conversation.	Tell students to ask themselves: What is the reason? (I'm late, I'm supposed to do something else, etc.).
3. Decide what to say.	Give students examples: "I have to go now, but I'll talk with you later." "I have to get back to my work." Students may want to suggest another time to continue the conversation.
4. Wait until the other person stops talking.	Discuss the importance of not interrupting and of thinking whether or not this is a good time to end the conversation.
5. Say it in a friendly way.	Remind students of the body language and nonverbal communicators that show a friendly attitude.

SUGGESTED SITUATIONS

School: Recess or free time in the classroom is over.

Home: You are talking with your parents, and a friend is waiting for you.

Peer group: Your mother tells you to come inside or stop talking on the telephone.

COMMENTS

This skill begins where Skill 15 (Beginning a Conversation) leaves off. After practicing each skill separately, give the students practice in using these skills successively.

GROUP II: FRIENDSHIP-MAKING SKILLS
Skill 17: Joining In

STEPS	NOTES FOR DISCUSSION
1. Decide if you want to join in.	Students should decide whether they really want to participate or whether they only want to disrupt the group.
2. Decide what to say.	Suggest possible things to say: "Can one more person play?" "Would it be okay with you if I played, too?"
3. Choose a good time.	Discuss how to choose a good time: during a break in the activity or before the activity has begun.
4. Say it in a friendly way.	Discuss the body language and nonverbal communicators that show a friendly attitude.

SUGGESTED SITUATIONS

School: Ask to join a group game at recess.

Home: Ask to join a game with parents or brothers and sisters.

Peer group: Ask to join an activity at a club or in the neighborhood.

COMMENTS

This skill is very useful for students who have difficulty deciding what to do in social play situations. This skill gives them the opportunity to join peers in an ongoing activity.

GROUP II: FRIENDSHIP-MAKING SKILLS
Skill 18: Playing a Game

STEPS	NOTES FOR DISCUSSION
1. Be sure you know the rules.	Discuss what to do if students don't know the rules (ask someone to explain them).
2. Decide who starts the game.	Discuss methods of deciding who begins the game: for example, roll the dice or offer to let the other person go first.
3. Remember to wait your turn.	Suggest that students repeat to themselves, "I can wait until it's my turn."
4. When the game is over, say something nice to the other person.	Discuss and practice appropriate ways of handling winning (tell the person he/she played a good game) and losing (congratulate the other person).

SUGGESTED SITUATIONS

School: Play a board game with a classmate or a group game at recess.

Home: Play a game with your parents, brother, or sister.

Peer group: Play a group game with friends in the neighborhood.

COMMENTS

It may be helpful to coach students in how to play a variety of games (e.g., classroom board games and group games played at recess or in the neighborhood) so that they will feel confident in playing the games. Posting lists of classroom games and recess games with which the students are familiar may also encourage them to play such acceptable games.

Good skills to teach following this one are Dealing with Losing (Skill 49) and Showing Sportsmanship (Skill 50).

GROUP II: FRIENDSHIP-MAKING SKILLS
SKILL 19: Asking a Favor

STEPS	NOTES FOR DISCUSSION
1. Decide if you want or need to ask a favor.	Discuss how to evaluate whether the favor is necessary.
2. Plan what you want to say.	Suggest things to say: "Could you help me with this?" "I can't see if I sit over there, would you mind making room for me?" "I'm having trouble getting my work done, would you please not talk?" Giving reasons for needing the favor may increase the chances that the person will help the student.
3. Ask the favor in a friendly way.	Discuss the body language and nonverbal communicators that show a friendly attitude.
4. Remember to thank the person.	Students should be taught the skill Saying Thank You (Skill 3).

SUGGESTED SITUATIONS

School: You would like to join a group and someone must move over to make room for you, or someone is making a noise that interferes with your work or bothers you.

Home: The television is too loud for you to do your homework.

Peer group: A friend is going to a movie and you'd like to go along, or you would like to borrow something of a friend's.

COMMENTS

The definition of a "favor," as used in this skill, is anything a student needs help with, varying from problems with other people to school and other informational problems.

It may be necessary to discuss what to do or say if the person can't do the favor for the student.

GROUP II: FRIENDSHIP-MAKING SKILLS
Skill 20: Offering Help to a Classmate

STEPS	NOTES FOR DISCUSSION
1. Decide if the person may need and want your help.	Discuss how to determine if another student needs help: How does he/she look? What is he/she doing or saying?
2. Think of what you may do to help.	Observing the person can help the student decide whether to offer physical help or verbal guidance.
3. Decide how to ask if you may help.	Discuss a variety of ways to offer help.
4. Ask yourself "Is this a good time to offer help?"	Remind students to be sure that they are not supposed to be doing something else.
5. Ask the person in a friendly way if you may help.	Discuss the body language and nonverbal communicators that show a friendly attitude. Emphasize not feeling hurt or offended if the person says no or asks someone else for help.
6. Help the person.	Discuss the importance of following through with help.

SUGGESTED SITUATIONS

School: A classmate drops his/her books or is having difficulty with a project.

Peer group: A friend is having difficulty painting his/her bicycle or completing a chore (e.g., carrying heavy boxes).

COMMENTS

A discussion of how people feel when helping someone or being helped should be included.

GROUP II: FRIENDSHIP-MAKING SKILLS
Skill 21: Giving a Compliment

STEPS	NOTES FOR DISCUSSION
1. Decide what you want to tell the other person.	Discuss the types of things students may want to compliment someone on: appearance, behavior, an achievement.
2. Decide how you want to say it.	Give examples of compliments.
3. Choose a good time and place.	Discuss how to choose a good time: when the student and the other person aren't busy, and perhaps when a lot of other people aren't around.
4. Give the compliment in a friendly way.	Emphasize giving the compliment in a sincere manner. Discuss the body language and facial expression associated with sincerity.

SUGGESTED SITUATIONS

School: A classmate has done really well on an assignment or has worked very hard on a project.

Home: Your mom or dad makes a good dinner.

Peer group: You like what someone is wearing.

COMMENTS

Emphasis should be placed on *sincerely* complimenting someone. This skill may appear mechanical and insincere when students first begin using it. Once they have sufficient practice with Giving a Compliment, the skill will be used in a more natural manner.

Discuss the way both the giver and recipient of the compliment would feel (e.g., embarrassed, pleased).

GROUP II: FRIENDSHIP-MAKING SKILLS
SKILL 22: Accepting a Compliment

STEPS	NOTES FOR DISCUSSION
1. Decide if someone has given you a compliment.	Discuss ways students can tell whether someone has given them a compliment; for instance, how the person looked and sounded when he/she made the comment.
2. Say thank you.	Students should be taught the skill Saying Thank You (Skill 3).
3. Say something else if you want to.	Give an example: "Yes, I tried hard." Suggest using the skill Beginning a Conversation (Skill 15).

SUGGESTED SITUATIONS

School: The teacher compliments you on work well done.

Home: Your parents compliment you on how well you did your chores.

Peer group: A friend compliments you on the way you look.

COMMENTS

This skill is important, as children are frequently embarrassed when given a compliment. Children with low self-esteem may also become defensive when given a compliment, as if they don't believe what the person is saying. Such a child may interpret the compliment as harrassment.

GROUP II: FRIENDSHIP-MAKING SKILLS
Skill 23: Suggesting an Activity

STEPS	NOTES FOR DISCUSSION
1. Decide on an activity you want to suggest.	Discuss a variety of appropriate activities to suggest in various settings (playground, during free time in the classroom, etc.).
2. Decide what you will say.	Give an example: "How would you like to _____?"
3. Choose a good time.	Discuss how to choose a good time: when others aren't involved with another activity.
4. Say it in a friendly way.	Discuss the body language and nonverbal communicators that show a friendly attitude.

SUGGESTED SITUATIONS

School: Suggest a group game during recess.

Home: Suggest an evening out with your parents (e.g., going to a movie).

Peer group: Suggest a game or an activity to a friend.

COMMENTS

Children may need to have experience with a variety of activities and games in order to be successful in suggesting activities. It may be helpful to coach students in how to play a variety of games. The activity needs to be appropriate to the setting (for example, the classroom versus the playground or neighborhood) and to the number of students involved (group versus individual).

Discuss what to say if someone says no to a suggested activity: Students should ask, "What would you like to do?" or go ask someone else to play.

GROUP II: FRIENDSHIP-MAKING SKILLS
Skill 24: Sharing

STEPS	NOTES FOR DISCUSSION
1. Decide if you want to share something.	Talk about how the other person might feel if the student does or doesn't share.
2. Decide whom you want to share with.	If the student can only share with one person, discuss how others around may feel left out.
3. Choose a good time and place.	Discuss how to choose a good time: when another person needs or would enjoy using something of the student's.
4. Offer to share in a friendly and sincere way.	Discuss the body language and facial expression associated with sincerity.

SUGGESTED SITUATIONS

School: Offer to share your materials (crayons, pencils, paper) with a classmate.

Home: Offer to share a treat with a friend, brother, or sister.

Peer group: Offer to share a game or toys with a friend.

GROUP II: FRIENDSHIP-MAKING SKILLS
SKILL 25: Apologizing

STEPS	NOTES FOR DISCUSSION
1. Decide if you need to apologize for something you did.	Discuss how we sometimes do things for which we are later sorry. Apologizing is something we can do to let the other person know we are sorry. It also often makes us feel better. Emphasize sincerity.
2. Think about your choices: a. Say it out loud to the person. b. Write the person a note.	Discuss when it is best to use verbal or written ways to apologize.
3. Choose a good time and place.	Discuss how to choose a good time: apologize soon after the problem. The student may want to be alone with the person for a verbal apology.
4. Carry out your best choice in a sincere way.	Discuss the body language and facial expression associated with sincerity.

SUGGESTED SITUATIONS

School: You are late for a class.

Home: You accidentally break something.

Peer group: You said something cruel because you were angry, or you had planned to do something with a friend but you have to go somewhere with your parents instead.

COMMENTS

It may be beneficial to discuss how difficult it might be to apologize. Discussion of how a person might feel before apologizing (e.g., anxious, afraid) as well as how a person might feel receiving the apology (e.g., relieved, less upset or angry) may make students more willing to try.

GROUP III: SKILLS FOR DEALING WITH FEELINGS
Skill 26: Knowing Your Feelings

STEPS	NOTES FOR DISCUSSION
1. Think of how your body feels.	Discuss the cues students' bodies may give them; for example, blushing, tight muscles, queasy stomach, or "jumpy" stomach.
2. Decide what you could call the feeling.	Discuss feelings such as frustration, fear, embarrassment, and their associated physical reactions.
3. Say to yourself "I feel _____."	

SUGGESTED SITUATIONS

School: You are frustrated with a difficult assignment.

Home: You are angry because your parents forgot to do something they had promised to do.

Peer group: You are disappointed because a friend promised to go to a movie with you, but he/she can't go.

COMMENTS

Additional activities specific to identifying and labeling feelings may need to be carried out. This might include generating a list of feeling words to be displayed in the classroom, along with pictures of persons expressing those feelings ("body talk").

GROUP III: SKILLS FOR DEALING WITH FEELINGS
Skill 27: Expressing Your Feelings

STEPS	NOTES FOR DISCUSSION
1. Stop and think of how you feel.	A list of feelings should be displayed in the classroom.
2. Decide what it is you are feeling.	Discuss how students can identify their feelings and what made them feel that way.
3. Think about your choices:	
a. Say to the person "I feel _____."	Consider when and where the student may be able to talk about the feeling.
b. Walk away for now.	Suggest this alternative as a way to calm down.
c. Get involved in an activity.	Discuss alternative activities.
4. Act out your best choice.	If the student is still angry after following these steps, he/she should wait until he/she isn't so angry before acting on the best choice. If one choice doesn't work, the student should try another one.

SUGGESTED SITUATIONS

School: You want to answer in class, but you're afraid your answer will be wrong.

Home: Your parents won't allow you to watch a movie on T.V. that many of your friends are going to watch.

Peer group: Someone calls you a name or ignores you.

COMMENTS

The teacher can model this behavior throughout the school year by expressing his/her feelings to the class in the appropriate manner.

GROUP III: SKILLS FOR DEALING WITH FEELINGS
SKILL 28: Recognizing Another's Feelings

STEPS	NOTES FOR DISCUSSION
1. Watch the person.	Discuss paying attention to the way the person looks (posture and facial expression), what the person does and says, and how he/she says it.
2. Name what you think the person is feeling.	A list of feeling words should be displayed in the classroom for reference.
3. Decide whether or not to ask the person if he/she is feeling that way.	If the person seems very angry or upset, it may be best for the student to wait until the person has calmed down.

SUGGESTED SITUATIONS

School: After assignments are handed back, a student starts to cry.

Home: Your dad or mom is slamming doors and muttering to himself/herself.

Peer group: A friend hasn't been chosen for a game, or a classmate just watches a game instead of asking to join.

COMMENTS

This skill should precede Showing Understanding of Another's Feelings (Skill 29).

GROUP III: SKILLS FOR DEALING WITH FEELINGS
Skill 29: Showing Understanding of Another's Feelings

STEPS	NOTES FOR DISCUSSION
1. Name what you think the person is feeling.	Discuss how the student might feel if he/she were in that situation.
2. Think about your choices:	Discuss how the student should base his/her choice on how well he/she knows the other person and the cues the person is giving.
a. Ask the person if he/she feels this way.	
b. Ask the person if you can help.	
c. Leave the person alone.	If the person seems very angry or upset, it may be best to leave the person alone for now and then make another choice when the person is less upset.
3. Act out your best choice.	If one choice doesn't work, the student should try another one.

SUGGESTED SITUATIONS

School: A classmate is crying because someone teased him/her.

Home: Your brother or sister won't talk to anyone after having a talk with a parent.

Peer group: A friend throws a board game after losing.

COMMENTS

Recognizing Another's Feelings (Skill 28) should be taught prior to this skill.

GROUP III: SKILLS FOR DEALING WITH FEELINGS
SKILL 30: Expressing Concern for Another

STEPS	NOTES FOR DISCUSSION
1. Decide if someone is having a problem.	Discuss ways to determine if someone is having a problem: What is the person doing? How does he/she look? Discuss how it might feel to be in that position.
2. Think about your choices:	
a. Say "Can I help you?"	Emphasize sincerity.
b. Do something nice for the person.	Suggest that the student share something with the person or ask the person to join in an activity.
3. Act out your best choice.	If one choice doesn't work, the student should try another one.

SUGGESTED SITUATIONS

School: A classmate is struggling with a difficult assignment.

Home: A parent is having difficulty with an activity.

Peer group: A friend has hurt himself/herself.

GROUP III: SKILLS FOR DEALING WITH FEELINGS
Skill 31: Dealing With Your Anger

STEPS	NOTES FOR DISCUSSION
1. Stop and count to ten.	Discuss the importance of allowing oneself time to cool off and think.
2. Think about your choices:	
a. Tell the person in words why you are angry.	Discuss how to tell the person in a way that won't anger him/her too.
b. Walk away for now.	Students may need to ask the teacher if they can leave the room and run an errand for him/her, or leave the classroom for 2–3 minutes.
c. Do a relaxation exercise.	Students should be taught the skill Relaxing (Skill 56).
3. Act out your best choice.	If one choice doesn't work, the student should try another one.

SUGGESTED SITUATIONS

School: You don't think the teacher has been fair to you, you are angry at yourself for forgetting your homework, or you are having a day where everything seems to go wrong.

Home: Your parents won't let you have a friend over or won't let you leave the house.

Peer group: A friend talks about you behind your back.

COMMENTS

For a child who directs anger toward himself/herself, additional choices may need to be included. Such choices may include: "Write about how you feel" or "Decide how you can change to keep this from happening again." Skills such as Problem Solving (Skill 41) can also assist many children who have difficulty dealing with their anger at themselves.

GROUP III: SKILLS FOR DEALING WITH FEELINGS
Skill 32: Dealing with Another's Anger

STEPS	NOTES FOR DISCUSSION
1. Listen to what the person has to say.	Discuss the importance of not interrupting or becoming defensive. If needed, the student should say to himself/herself, "I can stay calm."
2. Think about your choices:	Discuss the possible consequences of each choice.
a. Keep listening.	
b. Ask why he/she is angry.	
c. Give him/her an idea to fix the problem.	
d. Walk away for now.	If the student begins to feel angry too, he/she should walk away until he/she calms down.
3. Act out your best choice.	If one choice doesn't work, the student should try another one.

SUGGESTED SITUATIONS

School: The teacher is angry at you for not doing well on a test.

Home: Your parents are angry because you didn't clean your room.

Peer group: Another student is angry at you because you didn't choose him/her to play a game.

GROUP III: SKILLS FOR DEALING WITH FEELINGS
Skill 33: Expressing Affection

STEPS	NOTES FOR DISCUSSION
1. Decide if you have good feelings about the other person.	Discuss these feelings.
2. Decide if you think the other person would like to know you feel this way.	Discuss possible consequences of telling the person; for example, the person may become embarrassed, or it may make the person feel good.
3. Decide what you will say.	
4. Choose a good time and place.	Discuss how to choose a good time: Being alone may make it easier to express affection.
5. Tell the person in a friendly way.	Discuss the body language and nonverbal communicators that show a friendly attitude.

SUGGESTED SITUATIONS

School: Thank a teacher for something he/she has done.

Home: Tell your parents that you love them.

Peer group: Tell friends that you like them and want to continue being friends.

COMMENTS

This skill may be difficult for many adults to carry out, and therefore students may have had this skill modeled for them quite infrequently. It is important for the teacher to provide this type of modeling for the students.

GROUP III: SKILLS FOR DEALING WITH FEELINGS
Skill 34: Dealing with Fear

STEPS	NOTES FOR DISCUSSION
1. Decide if you are feeling afraid.	Discuss bodily cues of fear (e.g., sweaty hands or nausea).
2. Decide what you are afraid of.	Discuss real threats versus imagined ones. Students should ask themselves if the fear is a real threat to their physical safety. They may need to check this out with another person.
3. Think about your choices:	
a. Talk to someone about it.	Discuss choosing someone who can reassure you (teacher or parent).
b. Do a relaxation exercise.	Students should be taught the skill Relaxing (Skill 56).
c. Try what you are afraid of doing, anyway.	
4. Act out your best choice.	If one choice doesn't work, the student should try another one.

SUGGESTED SITUATIONS

School: You are afraid to take a test, or you are afraid to go out to recess because someone said he/she would beat you up.

Home: You are home alone at night.

Peer group: Someone in the neighborhood keeps teasing you.

COMMENTS

Students should be encouraged to evaluate realistic versus unrealistic fears. When fears are realistic ones, the alternative of talking to someone about them would be the suggested choice. Students may also need to problem solve ways to deal with realistic fears (see Skill 41: Problem Solving).

GROUP III: SKILLS FOR DEALING WITH FEELINGS
Skill 35: Rewarding Yourself

STEPS	NOTES FOR DISCUSSION
1. Decide if you did a good job.	Discuss ways to evaluate one's own performance.
2. Say to yourself "I did a good job."	
3. Decide how else you will reward yourself.	Give examples of other self-rewards: Ask if you can take a break, or do something you enjoy. Discuss these choices.
4. Do it.	Point out that students should reward themselves as soon after their performance as possible.

SUGGESTED SITUATIONS

School: You completed all of your assignments.

Home: You cleaned your room.

Peer group: You helped a friend do his/her chores.

COMMENTS

Emphasize that a person doesn't always have to depend on others to reward his/her actions.

GROUP IV: SKILL ALTERNATIVES TO AGGRESSION
Skill 36: Using Self-control

STEPS	NOTES FOR DISCUSSION
1. Stop and count to ten.	Discuss the importance of allowing oneself time to cool off and think.
2. Think of how your body feels.	Discuss how bodily cues may signal losing control (e.g., hands become sweaty, you feel hot).
3. Think about your choices:	
a. Walk away for now.	Students should ask to leave the room for a few minutes, if necessary, until they regain self-control.
b. Do a relaxation exercise.	Students should be taught the skill Relaxing (Skill 56).
c. Write about how you feel.	
d. Talk to someone about it.	Discuss choosing someone who would understand.
4. Act out your best choice.	If one choice doesn't work, the student should try another one.

SUGGESTED SITUATIONS

School: You are behind in your schoolwork.

Home: Your parents won't let you do what you want to do.

Peer group: A friend borrows something of yours and breaks it.

COMMENTS

This skill is to be used when the student is too angry or upset to identify what he/she is feeling and needs to control himself/herself first, rather than deal with the problem directly.

GROUP IV: SKILL ALTERNATIVES TO AGGRESSION
Skill 37: **Asking Permission**

STEPS	NOTES FOR DISCUSSION
1. Decide what you want to do.	Remind students to be sure this activity won't be harmful to themselves or another person.
2. Decide whom to ask.	This will usually be parents or teachers.
3. Decide what you will say.	
4. Choose the right time and place.	Discuss how to choose a good time: when the person isn't involved with another activity. The student may want to ask privately.
5. Ask in a friendly way.	Discuss the body language and nonverbal communicators that show a friendly attitude.

SUGGESTED SITUATIONS

School: Ask the teacher for a special privilege.

Home: Ask your parents if you may go to a friend's house or if you may participate in a school activity.

Peer group: Ask a friend if you may borrow a toy.

COMMENTS

We hope that the students' use of the skills presented in this volume will be successful the majority of the time. With this skill, however, many times permission may not be granted (e.g., parents can't afford it, friend's house is too far away). Therefore, if permission is not given (the skill does not work for the student), the skills of Rewarding Yourself (Skill 35) and/or Accepting No (Skill 54) should be taught immediately after instruction in this skill.

GROUP IV: SKILL ALTERNATIVES TO AGGRESSION
Skill 38: Responding to Teasing

STEPS	NOTES FOR DISCUSSION
1. Stop and count to five.	Discuss how this can prevent students from losing control.
2. Think about your choices:	
a. Ignore the teasing.	Point out that ignoring for a short time doesn't always work; the student may need to ignore for a long time. Discuss ways to ignore (e.g., walk away).
b. Say how you feel, in a friendly way.	Give an example of an "I feel" statement: "I feel _____ when _____."
c. Give a reason for the person to stop.	Suggest some possible reasons: the student will tell the teacher or another adult; the student is feeling uncomfortable, etc. Emphasize saying it in a friendly way.
3. Act out your best choice.	If one choice doesn't work, the student should try another one.

SUGGESTED SITUATIONS

School: Someone is poking you or making faces at you in class.

Home: Your brother or sister laughs at you.

Peer group: Someone calls you a name or teases you about your hair or clothes.

COMMENTS

The students may need practice in making appropriate, nonthreatening "I feel" statements.

GROUP IV: SKILL ALTERNATIVES TO AGGRESSION
Skill 39: Avoiding Trouble

STEPS	NOTES FOR DISCUSSION
1. Stop and think of what the consequences of an action might be.	It is helpful to list and discuss the possible consequences of particular actions with the students.
2. Decide if you want to stay out of trouble.	Discuss how to decide if it is important to avoid these consequences.
3. Decide what to tell the other person.	
4. Tell the person.	Discuss how to say no in a friendly but firm way.

SUGGESTED SITUATIONS

School: Another student wants you to help him/her cheat on a test.

Home: Your brother or sister wants you to take money from your parents.

Peer group: A friend wants you to tease another friend.

COMMENTS

It is important to teach students to anticipate the consequences of their actions. They may still choose to accept these consequences.

GROUP IV: SKILL ALTERNATIVES TO AGGRESSION
Skill 40: Staying Out of Fights

STEPS	NOTES FOR DISCUSSION
1. Stop and count to ten.	Discuss how this can help the student to calm down.
2. Decide what the problem is.	Discuss the consequences of fighting, and whether fighting can solve a problem.
3. Think about your choices:	List a variety of alternatives.
a. Walk away for now.	Students should ask to leave the room for a few minutes, if necessary.
b. Talk to the person in a friendly way.	Discuss how to read the behavior of the other person (i.e., is he/she calm enough to talk with) and evaluate one's own degree of calmness and readiness to talk about the problem. Discuss ways to state the problem in a nonoffensive manner.
c. Ask someone for help in solving the problem.	Discuss who can be of the most help: a teacher, parent, or friend.
4. Act out your best choice.	If one choice doesn't work, the student should try another one.

SUGGESTED SITUATIONS

School: Someone says that you did poorly on your schoolwork.

Home: Your brother or sister tattles on you.

Peer group: Someone doesn't play fairly in a game or calls you a name.

GROUP IV: SKILL ALTERNATIVES TO AGGRESSION
SKILL 41: Problem Solving

STEPS	NOTES FOR DISCUSSION
1. Stop and say "I have to calm down."	Discuss additional ways to calm down (e.g., take three deep breaths, count to ten).
2. Decide what the problem is.	Discuss how students should reflect on why they are upset.
3. Think about different ways to solve the problem.	List and discuss a variety of alternatives and the consequences of each.
4. Choose one way.	Discuss how to weigh alternatives to pick the best.
5. Do it.	
6. Ask yourself "How did this work?"	If one alternative doesn't work, the student should try another.

SUGGESTED SITUATIONS

School: You don't understand an assignment, or you forgot your
         lunch money.

Home: You broke a window at your house.

Peer group: You lost something you borrowed from a friend.

COMMENTS

As problems arise in the classroom, it may be beneficial if the
teacher leads the class in a discussion of the alternatives to deal with
the problem and the possible consequences of each alternative. By
listing and discussing these alternatives and consequences, the
students can choose the best one for them. Using this problem-
solving technique when classroom problems arise will promote the
students' ability to use this skill and will also teach them *when* the
skill can be used.
   This is a good prerequisite skill for Accepting Consequences
(Skill 42).

GROUP IV: SKILL ALTERNATIVES TO AGGRESSION
Skill 42: Accepting Consequences

STEPS	NOTES FOR DISCUSSION
1. Decide if you were wrong.	Discuss that it is okay to be wrong . . . it's not the end of the world.
2. If you were wrong, say to yourself "I have to accept the consequences."	Discuss the possible consequences of particular actions.
3. Say to the person "Yes, I did _____" (describe what you did).	Discuss how to describe the *behavior* without making excuses.
4. Say something else:	
a. How you will avoid this behavior the next time.	Point out that this should be said in a friendly manner.
b. Apologize.	Emphasize sincerity.

SUGGESTED SITUATIONS

School: You forgot your homework assignment.

Home: Your parents tell you that you can't go to a movie because you didn't do your chores.

Peer group: You lost the money your friend asked you to keep for him/her.

COMMENTS

Since this skill involves some problem solving, it is suggested that this skill be taught after Problem Solving (Skill 41).

GROUP IV: SKILL ALTERNATIVES TO AGGRESSION
Skill 43: Dealing with an Accusation

STEPS	NOTES FOR DISCUSSION
1. Stop and say "I have to calm down."	Discuss additional ways to calm down (e.g., take three deep breaths, count to ten).
2. Think about what the person has accused you of.	
3. Ask yourself "Is the person right?"	If the student decides that the person is correct, the skill Accepting Consequences (Skill 42) can be used.
4. Think about your choices:	
a. Explain, in a friendly way, that you didn't do it.	Discuss the body language and nonverbal communicators that show a friendly attitude.
b. Apologize.	Emphasize sincerity.
c. Offer to make up for what happened.	Discuss how to make amends: earning the money to pay for a lost or broken item; giving the person something of one's own; or giving back a stolen item to the person.
5. Act out your best choice.	If one choice doesn't work, the student should try another one.

SUGGESTED SITUATIONS

School: A teacher has accused you of cheating.

Home: Your parents accuse you of breaking something.

Peer group: A friend accuses you of taking something that wasn't yours.

GROUP IV: SKILL ALTERNATIVES TO AGGRESSION
Skill 44: Negotiating

STEPS	NOTES FOR DISCUSSION
1. Decide if you and the other person disagree.	Discuss signs of disagreement: Is the student getting angry? Is the other person getting angry?
2. Tell how you feel about the problem.	Discuss the importance of saying this in a friendly way, so the other person does not become more angry.
3. Ask the person how he/she feels about the problem.	
4. Listen to the answer.	Discuss the importance of not interrupting.
5. Suggest or ask for a compromise.	Discuss how to decide on something that will satisfy both the student and the other person.

SUGGESTED SITUATIONS

School: Your teacher gives you work that you feel you can't do.

Home: Your parents want you to baby-sit, but you need to do your homework.

Peer group: Your friend wants to play one game, but you want to play another.

COMMENTS

This skill may be difficult for the very young child and is considered to be more appropriate for students in grades four and five.

GROUP V: SKILLS FOR DEALING WITH STRESS
Skill 45: Dealing with Boredom

STEPS	NOTES FOR DISCUSSION
1. Decide if you are feeling bored.	Discuss how to recognize signs of boredom (e.g., you don't know what to do; you feel jittery inside).
2. Think of things you like to do.	Students should generate and discuss personal lists of acceptable activities.
3. Decide on one thing to do.	
4. Do it.	
5. Say to yourself "Good for me. I chose something to do."	Discuss ways of rewarding oneself.

SUGGESTED SITUATIONS

School: There are no playground games you are interested in.

Home: It's a Saturday and no one is around.

Peer group: You and your friends can't think of anything to do.

COMMENTS

This skill, similar to Deciding on Something to Do (Skill 12), is geared for use outside of the academic learning setting. It is suggested that the students generate a list of acceptable activities they may engage in on the playground, at home, and in the neighborhood, and include these lists in their prosocial skills folder.

Self-reward (Step 5) is a skill (Skill 35) that may provide the student with necessary reinforcement until the skill can be reinforced by the teacher or parent.

GROUP V: SKILLS FOR DEALING WITH STRESS
Skill 46: Deciding What Caused a Problem

STEPS	NOTES FOR DISCUSSION
1. Decide what the problem is.	Discuss how students can recognize a problem: by the way they feel inside; by what someone said to them ; or by how someone acted toward them.
2. Think about what may have caused the problem.	Discuss how to evaluate possible causes of a problem: one's own behavior; someone else's behavior; or no one's fault.
3. Decide what most likely caused the problem.	Discuss how to determine the most likely cause.
4. Check it out.	Ask someone, either the other person or an impartial judge.

SUGGESTED SITUATIONS

School: The teacher seems angry with you.

Home: Your parents have an argument about you.

Peer group: You feel angry at a friend, but don't know why, or you feel that someone doesn't like you.

COMMENTS

This skill is intended to help students distinguish the problems that they are responsible for and those that are due to factors outside of their control.

GROUP V: SKILLS FOR DEALING WITH STRESS
Skill 47: Making a Complaint

STEPS	NOTES FOR DISCUSSION
1. Decide what the problem is.	Discuss how students can recognize a problem: by the way they feel inside; by what someone said to them; or by how someone acted toward them.
2. Decide whom to tell.	Students should decide whom they are having the problem with. Talking about the problem with the person should help solve it.
3. Choose a good time and place.	Discuss how to choose a good time: when the person isn't involved with something else, or when the person is alone.
4. Tell the person your problem in a friendly way.	Tell students to wait until they are no longer angry or upset before talking about the problem. Discuss the body language and nonverbal communicators that show a friendly attitude.

SUGGESTED SITUATIONS

School: The teacher gives you an assignment that seems too difficult for you.

Home: You feel your parents were unfair because they wouldn't let you go to a movie with a friend.

Peer group: A friend usually chooses what the two of you will do.

GROUP V: SKILLS FOR DEALING WITH STRESS
Skill 48: Answering a Complaint

STEPS	NOTES FOR DISCUSSION
1. Listen to the complaint.	Discuss proper body language while listening: ways to *show* that you aren't defensive.
2. Ask in a friendly way about anything you don't understand.	Discuss the body language and nonverbal communicators that show a friendly attitude.
3. Decide if the complaint is justified.	
4. Think about your choices:	
a. Apologize.	Emphasize sincerity.
b. Explain your behavior.	Discuss that even if a student did not intend to cause a problem, his/her behavior still might have caused a problem for someone else.
c. Suggest what to do now.	
d. Correct a mistaken impression.	Discuss how to respond to an unjustified complaint by explaining why it is wrong.
5. Act out your best choice.	If one choice doesn't work, the student should try another one.

SUGGESTED SITUATIONS

School: The teacher complains that you are too loud.

Home: Your parents complain that you haven't helped at home.

Peer group: A friend complains that you were teasing him/her.

GROUP V: SKILLS FOR DEALING WITH STRESS
SKILL 49: Dealing with Losing

STEPS	NOTES FOR DISCUSSION
1. Say to yourself "Somebody has to lose. It's okay that I didn't win."	Memorizing this statement will act as an impulse-control technique for the student.
2. Think about your choices:	
a. Ask to help someone.	Offer help to the teacher or your parents.
b. Do an activity you like to do.	Students should generate and discuss personal lists of acceptable activities.
c. Do a relaxation exercise.	Students should be taught the skill Relaxing (Skill 56).
3. Act out your best choice.	If one choice doesn't work, the student should try another one.

SUGGESTED SITUATIONS

School: You lose a contest or a raffle.

Home: You lose at a game with your brother or sister.

Peer group: Your team loses at basketball (or some other game).

COMMENTS

This is a good prerequisite skill for Showing Sportmanship (Skill 50).

GROUP V: SKILLS FOR DEALING WITH STRESS
Skill 50: Showing Sportsmanship

STEPS	NOTES FOR DISCUSSION
1. Decide how you and the other person played the game.	Discuss evaluating one's own level of skill and an opponent's.
2. Think of what you can honestly tell the other person or group:	Emphasize sincerity in what the student chooses to say.
a. Congratulations.	The student may also want to shake the person's hand.
b. You played a good game.	
c. You're getting a lot better at this game.	
3. Act out your best choice.	Discuss the body language and nonverbal communicators that show a friendly, sincere attitude.
4. Help the other person put the game or materials away.	

SUGGESTED SITUATIONS

School: Your team loses at a group game during recess, or your team wins.

Home: You lose at a game with your brother or sister, or you win.

Peer group: You lose at a game with a friend, or you win.

COMMENTS

Students should be taught the skill Dealing with Losing (Skill 49) before this one.

GROUP V: SKILLS FOR DEALING WITH STRESS
Sᴋɪʟʟ 51: Dealing with Being Left Out

STEPS	NOTES FOR DISCUSSION
1. Decide what has happened to cause you to feel left out.	Discuss possible reasons why a student may be ignored by peers.
2. Think about your choices:	
a. Ask to join in.	Students should be taught the skill Joining In (Skill 17).
b. Choose someone else to play with.	
c. Do an activity you enjoy.	Students should generate and discuss personal lists of acceptable activities.
3. Act out your best choice.	If one choice doesn't work, the student should try another one.

SUGGESTED SITUATIONS

School: You are left out of a group game at recess.

Home: Your brother or sister is leaving you out of an activity with his/her friends.

Peer group: A group of friends are going to a movie or a birthday party, but you weren't invited.

COMMENTS

It may be important to discuss the types of feelings that might result from being left out (feeling angry, hurt, or frustrated). When discussing this skill, the teacher might emphasize that it is important to deal with being left out through these skill steps, rather than to continue to feel angry or hurt.

GROUP V: SKILLS FOR DEALING WITH STRESS
Skill 52: Dealing with Embarrassment

STEPS	NOTES FOR DISCUSSION
1. Decide what happened to cause you to feel embarrassed.	Discuss how students can recognize signs of embarrassment (e.g., face feels flushed).
2. Think of what you can do to feel less embarrassed.	Discuss the possible consequences of each choice.
a. Ignore it.	
b. Decide what to do next time.	
c. Say to yourself "It's over. People will forget it."	
3. Act out your best choice.	If one choice doesn't work, the student should try another one.

SUGGESTED SITUATIONS

School: You give the wrong answer to a question in class.

Home: You drop and break something of your parents'.

Peer group: You fall down on the playground or make some other mistake when playing a game.

COMMENTS

Prior to teaching this skill, it is helpful to review Knowing Your Feelings (Skill 26).

GROUP V: SKILLS FOR DEALING WITH STRESS
Skill 53: Reacting to Failure

STEPS	NOTES FOR DISCUSSION
1. Decide if you have failed.	Discuss the difference between failing and not doing as well as hoped.
2. Think about why you failed.	Discuss reasons for failure: the student didn't try as hard as he/she could have; he/she wasn't ready to do this; it was a matter of chance.
3. Think about what you could do next time.	Suggest practicing more, trying harder, or asking for help.
4. Make your plan to do this.	This plan may be in written form such as a contingency contract.

SUGGESTED SITUATIONS

School: You failed a test.

Home: You failed to complete your chores at home.

Peer group: You failed to get someone to join in the activity you
wanted to do.

GROUP V: SKILLS FOR DEALING WITH STRESS
SKILL 54: Accepting No

STEPS	NOTES FOR DISCUSSION
1. Decide why you were told no.	Discuss the possible reasons for being told no in a particular situation.
2. Think about your choices:	Discuss the possible consequences of each choice.
a. Do something else.	Students should generate and discuss personal lists of acceptable activities.
b. Say how you feel, in a friendly way.	Practice "I feel" statements with the students. Discuss the body language and nonverbal communicators that show a friendly attitude.
c. Write about how you feel.	
3. Act out your best choice.	If one choice doesn't work, the student should try another one.

SUGGESTED SITUATIONS

School: The teacher says that you can't do an activity.

Home: Your parents say that you can't stay up late.

Peer group: A friend tells you he/she won't come over to your house.

COMMENTS

The choice "Write about how you feel" may not be appropriate for the very young child or the special education student who may not have such writing skills. Ask these students to generate other choices instead.

GROUP V: SKILLS FOR DEALING WITH STRESS
SKILL 55: Saying No

STEPS	NOTES FOR DISCUSSION
1. Decide whether or not you want to do what is being asked.	Discuss situations when saying no is appropriate.
2. Think about why you don't want to do this.	Discuss reasons for saying no: the student may get into trouble, or he/she has something else he/she wants to do.
3. Tell the person no in a friendly way.	Discuss the body language and nonverbal communicators that show a friendly attitude.
4. Give your reason why you won't do what the person asked.	Remind students that this, too, should be said in a friendly way.

SUGGESTED SITUATIONS

School: A friend wants you to run away from school with him/her.

Home: Your brother or sister wants you to play a game, but you want to watch your favorite T.V. program.

Peer group: A friend wants you to play when you have work to do, or he/she wants you to go to a movie after school, but you'd rather play baseball.

GROUP V: SKILLS FOR DEALING WITH STRESS
SKILL 56: Relaxing

STEPS	NOTES FOR DISCUSSION
1. Decide if you need to relax.	Discuss how to recognize bodily cues of tension (e.g., feeling tense or jittery inside, or feeling one's stomach churning).
2. Take three slow, deep breaths.	
3. Tighten one part of your body; count to three; relax.	Instruct students about which parts of their bodies to tighten/relax.
4. Continue this for each part of your body.	Steps 3 and 4 will take much practice.
5. Ask yourself how you feel.	Discuss how the students feel physically before and after tightening muscles.

SUGGESTED SITUATIONS

School: You feel nervous before a test.

Home: Your grandparents are coming and you're excited.

Peer group: You are angry or upset with a friend, but you don't
know why.

COMMENTS

Students may need a great deal of training in relaxation before they
will be able to use this skill effectively. A useful source for this
purpose is Bernstein and Borkovec (1973).

GROUP V: SKILLS FOR DEALING WITH STRESS
SKILL 57: Dealing with Group Pressure

STEPS	NOTES FOR DISCUSSION
1. Listen to what others want you to do.	Discuss possible reasons why the group may want the student to participate in particular actions.
2. Think about what might happen.	Discuss possible consequences of particular actions: someone may be hurt, or the student may get into trouble.
3. Decide what you want to do.	Discuss how difficult it is to resist pressure to do something from a group of friends.
4. If you decide not to go along with the group, say to them "No, I can't because _____" (give the reason).	Discuss how giving a reason for not going along may help the group to think about what they want to do.
5. Suggest something else to do.	Students should generate and discuss a list of acceptable group activities.

SUGGESTED SITUATIONS

Peer group: The group is teasing someone or planning on taking something that belongs to someone else, and they want you to go along with them.

GROUP V: SKILLS FOR DEALING WITH STRESS
SKILL 58: Dealing with Wanting Something That Isn't Mine

STEPS	NOTES FOR DISCUSSION
1. Say to yourself "I want this, but I can't just take it."	Discuss how hard it may be to want something and not take it.
2. Say "It belongs to _____."	Discuss how the other person might feel if the item were gone.
3. Think about your choices: a. I could ask to borrow it. b. I could earn the money to buy it. c. I could ask the person to trade.	Discuss other alternatives depending upon the possibilities for your students to get what they want.
d. I could do something else I like to do.	Students should generate and discuss personal lists of acceptable activities.
4. Act out your best choice.	If one choice doesn't work, the student should try another one.
5. Say "Good for me. I didn't take it!"	Discuss ways of rewarding oneself.

SUGGESTED SITUATIONS

School: You see a notebook you'd really like to have.

Home: Your parents left money on the table.

Peer group: A friend has a game you would like to have, or he/she has candy in his/her coat hanging in his/her locker.

COMMENTS

Step 5 of this skill will be a crucial step for many children. Because observers may not know that the student actually wanted to take something but succeeded in controlling himself/herself, outside reinforcement is unlikely to be given. Therefore, the student must learn to give himself/herself this needed reinforcement.

GROUP V: SKILLS FOR DEALING WITH STRESS
Skill 59: Making a Decision

STEPS	NOTES FOR DISCUSSION
1. Think about the problem.	Discuss how students may face conflicting desires or responsibilities at odds with desires.
2. Decide on your choices.	Have students make a list of the alternatives.
3. Think of the possible consequences for each choice.	Have students make a list of the consequences of each alternative and then discuss them.
4. Make the best decision.	Discuss how to evaluate competing alternatives to make the best choice.

SUGGESTED SITUATIONS

School: Decide what group to play with.

Home: Decide how to spend your money.

Peer group: Decide whether to go to a movie or stay home and study for a test.

GROUP V: SKILLS FOR DEALING WITH STRESS
Skill 60: Being Honest

STEPS	NOTES FOR DISCUSSION
1. Decide what might happen if you are honest.	Discuss politeness versus honesty: Students should not be honest just to hurt someone, such as saying that they don't like a person's clothes, for example. Also discuss how others may respect the student or trust the student more in the future if he/she is honest now.
2. Decide what might happen if you aren't honest.	Discuss how punishing consequences are usually less severe if a person is honest in the beginning.
3. Think of how to say what you have to say.	Give examples: "I'm sorry, but I did _____"; "Yes, I did it, but I didn't mean to."
4. Say it.	Emphasize sincerity.
5. Say to yourself "Good for me. I told the truth."	Discuss ways of rewarding oneself.

SUGGESTED SITUATIONS

School: You tore up your homework assignment or lost your reading book.

Home: You broke a window playing baseball.

Peer group: You borrowed someone's bike without asking permission.

COMMENTS

Self-reward (Step 5) is a skill (Skill 35) that may provide the student with necessary reinforcement until the skill can be reinforced by the teacher or parent.

CHAPTER 7

Structured Learning in Use: A Transcript

THE SESSION

The following is an edited transcript of a Structured Learning session with elementary-age mildly handicapped (behaviorally disordered) children. The group consists of two leaders and eight students. The goals for this session included enhancing student motivation to learn the session's skill, formulating the behavioral steps of the skill Dealing with Your Anger, and using Structured Learning to teach the skill.

ENHANCING MOTIVATION

Ms. Benson:	Today we are going to talk about a problem that someone in the group is having . . . and maybe more than one person has this problem. And that is, what to do when I'm angry. Do any of you have to deal with being angry?
Tom:	Yeah. Me and my brother fight a lot. Sometimes my brother makes me mad and sometimes I make him mad.
Ms. Benson:	Is dealing with your anger a skill you'd like to work on then?
Tom:	Yeah. 'Cause then I get in trouble with my mom.
Ms. Benson:	That's no fun, is it? Does anyone else sometimes have a hard time dealing with their anger?
Michelle:	Bill is always knocking my papers off my desk. He makes me mad!

Bill:	I do not!
Ms. Benson:	Michelle, what do you do then?
Michelle:	I yell at him to stop it or I'll tell the teacher.
Mr. Jennings:	Michelle, what happens when you yell at Bill?
Michelle:	The teacher gets mad at me, 'cause I bother the other kids working.
Chris:	I get mad when somebody says something they shouldn't say to me.

FORMULATING THE SKILL STEPS

Ms. Benson:	Okay, what do you do when someone says something to you that you don't like?
Chris:	I try to ignore them, but they keep saying it.
Ms. Benson:	Ignoring is one thing that you can do. Let's talk about when you're feeling really angry. What's the first thing that you should do when you're angry?
Steve:	Go out in the hall.
Mr. Jennings:	Why would you go out in the hall—what would that do for you?
Steve:	It gets you away from the class.
Mr. Jennings:	Good. It's a way to calm you down. When you're angry the first thing you need to do is stop and calm down. (Writes this on the board.) And what's something else you can do to calm down?
	(No response)
Ms. Benson:	What about counting to ten? Would that help you calm down?
Tammy:	Yeah. It gives me something else to think about.
Ms. Benson:	Good, Tammy. Counting to yourself is another good way to calm down. Then you can think of your choices. (Adds counting to ten to Step 1. Writes "Step 2: Think of your choices.")
Chris:	Outside when somebody tries to pick a fight with you the best thing to do is walk away.
Ms. Benson:	Good, Chris, that's one choice you could make. (Writes "Walk away" on the board under Step 2.)
Bill:	You can cry.

Ms. Benson:	Does crying solve your anger?
Bill:	No . . . sometimes.
Ms. Benson:	Crying can get the tension out—it can make you feel better. That's one thing you could do when you walk away. What else could you do to deal with your anger?
Tom:	Forget about it.
Ms. Benson:	You could forget about it, but sometimes that's easier to say than it is to do. When you're feeling really angry can you forget about it easily?
Michelle:	No! I stay mad.
Ms. Benson:	If you can forget about it, that might be okay. But if you're going to stay mad . . . if it keeps bugging you, what could you do?
Chris:	I usually try to read a book . . . it makes me think I'm in that world.
Ms. Benson:	You could get involved in something else—something you like to do, like reading a book—when you walk away from what has made you angry. (Writes this on the chalkboard under Step 2.) What else could you do?
Bill:	You should just forget about it.
Ms. Benson:	That might work for you. But what if someone can't forget about it. What if something keeps happening that causes you to feel angry and you have tried to forget about it, but the situation keeps coming up and you keep feeling angry?
Willie:	Try to relax.
Ms. Benson:	You could do a relaxation exercise. (Lists relaxation as a choice.) Any more ideas?
Jenny:	You could talk to somebody . . . or the person you're mad at.
Ms. Benson:	Right, you could talk to the person about why you're angry. And how would you talk to that person . . . would you talk in a mean, angry way? (Writes "Talk to the person.")
Tom:	No . . . then they will be mad.
Michelle:	You have to be nice.

Ms. Benson:	Yes, you'd try talking in a friendly way. (Adds this to "Talk to the person.") You came up with some very good choices. And after you decide what you're going to do, what then?
Bill:	You do it.
Ms. Benson:	Right, Bill. That's Step 3. You do it, or act out your best choice. (Writes this on the board.) The steps look like this:

Skill: Dealing with Your Anger
Steps: 1. Stop and count to ten.
        2. Think of your choices:
           a. Walk away.
           b. Do something you like to do.
           c. Try to relax.
           d. Talk to the person in a friendly way.
        3. Act out your best choice.

MODELING

Mr. Jennings:	Okay, we have the steps to the skill of Dealing with Your Anger. And many of you came up with problems you have where Dealing with Anger could help you. Tom, you get in trouble with your mom. Chris, you've tried ignoring and that hasn't seemed to work for you. And Michelle, you said that when you get mad and yell, then you get in trouble. Ms. Benson and I are going to act out the skill steps to Dealing with Your Anger. Ms. Benson will be sitting at this desk working and I'll walk by her desk. I'm going to knock her papers on the floor. I want you to all watch very carefully to see if Ms. Benson follows all the steps. What is the first step Ms. Benson needs to do?
Tammy:	(Looking at the steps written on the chalkboard.) Stop and count to ten.
Mr. Jennings:	Good. The next step.
Willie:	Think of your choices.
Mr. Jennings:	Yes. And what are her choices?
Chris:	Talk to the person in a friendly way.
Mr. Jennings:	Good. Other choices?
Steve:	Walk away.

Michelle:	Try to relax.
Bill:	Do something you like to do.
	(The students read these choices from the chalkboard.)
Mr. Jennings:	Good. What's the third step?
Tammy:	Act out your best choice.
Mr. Jennings:	Great. Now, let's watch to see if Ms. Benson follows all the steps. (Ms. Benson is sitting at a desk near the group and begins to work. Mr. Jennings walks by and knocks her papers to the floor.)
Ms. Benson:	He did it again. (She sighs.) Boy, that makes me angry! But I won't let him know that he's getting to me. So, first I have to stop and count to ten. One . . . two . . . three . . . four . . . five . . . six . . . seven . . . eight . . . nine . . . ten. Now I think of my choices. I could walk away, but he's done this before and I've already tried that. I could do something I like to do, but I have to get this work done. I think I'll try talking to him. Maybe if I tell him I have to get my work done, he'll stop doing this. Mr. Jennings, I've been trying to get this work done and now my papers are all messed up. Would you help me pick them up so I can get this project done?
Mr. Jennings:	Oh, well, I'm sorry. I guess I did mess things up for you.
Ms. Benson:	Yes, but I'd appreciate it if you'd help me.
Mr. Jennings:	Okay . . . sorry. (He assists Ms. Benson in picking up her papers.)
Ms. Benson:	Well, how did I do? Did I follow the first step?
Chris:	Yeah. You counted to ten.
Mr. Jennings:	Yes, you did a great job of stopping and counting to ten to control your anger. Did she follow Step 2?
Tom:	Yes.
Mr. Jennings:	How do you know?
Tom:	She said she was thinking about what to do.
Mr. Jennings:	Good. She thought about her choices out loud so we would know what she was thinking. What about Step 3?

| Michelle: | Yeah. She talked to you . . . told you why she was mad. |
| Mr. Jennings: | Right. Overall, how did Ms. Benson do? |

(Several students respond with "good.")
(A second modeling display is presented.)

ELICITING ROLE-PLAY SCENES

Ms. Benson:	Now, let's talk about how you might use this skill. Do you see some ways you could use this skill to deal with your anger?
Tom:	Yeah! When my little brother hits me.
Michelle:	When Bill pushes my stuff off on the floor . . . he always does that.
Steve:	My dad gets mad at me when I don't do my chores. Then I get mad.
Chris:	I get mad when that dumb science teacher gives me so much work to do.

PREPARING FOR THE ROLE PLAY

Ms. Benson:	Okay, there are lots of times we can use this skill to help deal with our anger. Who would like to try out this skill first?
Chris:	I would.
Ms. Benson:	Okay, Chris. Tell us more about what happens when you get angry at the science teacher.
Chris:	Well . . . you see . . . Mr. Gleason says I have to do all this stuff.
Mr. Jennings:	What kind of stuff?
Chris:	You see, we have to read this stuff in science . . . and answer these questions. He doesn't help me.
Ms. Benson:	Why can't you do the work, Chris?
Chris:	It's too much! And I get mad and sit . . . I don't do it!
Ms. Benson:	Then what might Mr. Gleason do?
Chris:	He tells me to go out in the hall. Then I *really* get mad 'cause the kids go by and laugh at me.
Mr. Jennings:	How does Mr. Gleason talk to you, Chris?
Chris:	What do you mean?

Mr. Jennings:	Well, is he friendly when he tells you to go out in the hall?
Chris:	No. He's mad.
Mr. Jennings:	Okay. When you're supposed to be working, are you sitting at your desk?
Chris:	Yeah.
Mr. Jennings:	All right then. Let's go over to this desk. (The group then moves to the classroom area, pulls chairs to the side, and sits to wait.) Here's a science book—is this the book you use?
Chris:	Yeah.
Mr. Jennings:	Where is Mr. Gleason when you're supposed to be working?
Chris:	He stands up there. (Points toward the chalkboard.)
Ms. Benson:	What are you discussing in science class?
Chris:	Plants and stuff.
Ms. Benson:	Good. I think we have a good idea of what happens. Who in the group reminds you most of Mr. Gleason?
Chris:	(Looking around the group.) Mr. Jennings, I guess. 'Cause he's a man, too.
Ms. Benson:	All right. Mr. Jennings, will you take the role of Mr. Gleason?
Mr. Jennings:	Sure.
Ms. Benson:	Now, let's review the skill steps. And I'll write them here so that Chris can look at them as he acts out the skill. (Ms. Benson elicits each skill step from the group and writes the steps so that Chris and the rest of the group can see them.)
Mr. Jennings:	Now, what could Chris do first?
Willie:	Stop and count to ten.
Mr. Jennings:	Good, Willie. Thanks for participating. What could he do then?
Steve:	He could tell Mr. Gleason why he's mad.
Michelle:	Yeah. That's what he should do. 'Cause if he walks away, he won't get his work done. Then he'll get in trouble.

Ms. Benson: Good thinking, Michelle. The choice of walking away in this situation may get Chris into more trouble. What could Chris say to Mr. Gleason?

Tammy: He could say he can't answer the questions.

Mr. Jennings: Thanks, Tammy. Then what could he do?

Bill: He could say he needs help.

Mr. Jennings: Okay. Chris, what do you think of these suggestions?

Chris: Yeah.

Mr. Jennings: Have you decided what you're going to do?

Chris: Yeah. I'm going to tell him why I'm mad . . . that I need help.

Mr. Jennings: How will you say it, Chris?

Chris: Well, I'd have to raise my hand, or he'd get mad.

Mr. Jennings: Good. Then what?

Chris: I could say I just get mad 'cause I can't do all of this.

Mr. Jennings: Okay . . . and then could you say anything else?

Chris: (Looks at Mr. Jennings as if confused.)

Ms. Benson: Does anyone have an idea of what Chris could say next?

Willie: He could ask Mr. Gleason to help him.

Ms. Benson: That's an idea, Willie. Chris, what do you think about doing that?

Chris: Yeah. I guess so.

Ms. Benson: If you want to ask for help, how could you ask for help?

Chris: I could say: I need help.

Ms. Benson: Do you think Mr. Gleason would help you then?

Chris: Yeah. If I don't sound mad.

ROLE PLAYING

Ms. Benson: I think we're ready to try it. Chris, are you ready?

Chris: Yeah.

Ms. Benson: We want to hear you do your thinking, Chris. So you'll have to think out loud. Mr. Jennings, you're in the role of Mr. Gleason and will be giving a science assignment. Chris, you are in science class. Follow the steps to Dealing with Your Anger . . . you can look at the board as you need to. Will you watch and see if Chris follows Step 1, Steve? Step 2, Bill; Step 3, Jenny. The rest of us will watch to see if he follows the steps, too, and we'll be watching to see if he talks in a friendly way and if his body talk is friendly, too. Ready?

(Group members indicate that they are ready; Ms. Benson positions herself at the chalkboard.)

Mr. Jennings: (Gleason)	Today we have talked about what plants need to survive and how to take care of them. Open to page 56 of your science book. (Chris opens his book.) Now, there are five questions. I want you to read the questions and write your answers. When you're finished, hand them in. Be sure to write your answers in complete sentences.
Chris:	(Looks at the science page, does nothing.)
Mr. Jennings: (Gleason)	Chris, get started on your assignment, please.
Chris:	(Takes out paper and a pencil from the desk, looks at the questions.)
Ms. Benson:	What are you thinking, Chris?
Chris:	I don't know the answers.
Ms. Benson:	Think about how you feel . . . you've just been given your science assignment, and you don't know the answers.
Chris:	I'm mad that I have to do it.
Ms. Benson:	So what will you do? (Points to the first step of the skill.)
Chris:	Stop and count to ten.
Ms. Benson:	Okay, count out loud.
Chris:	One . . . two . . . three . . . four . . . five . . . six . . . seven . . . eight . . . nine . . . ten. (Ms. Benson moves her hand to Step 2.)

I think of my choices. I could talk to him. I could walk away. No, I can't do that. I could try to relax, but it won't help me answer the questions. I guess I should talk to him and ask him to help. (Ms. Benson moves her hand to Step 3. Chris raises his hand.)

Mr. Jennings: Chris, what is it?
(Gleason)

Chris: I don't know the answers. Will you help me?

Mr. Jennings: Okay, what is the question?
(Gleason)
(Chris reads the question.)

Let's see if we can find the answer in the chapter.

PROVIDING PERFORMANCE FEEDBACK

Ms. Benson: Mr. Gleason, how did you feel about what Chris did?

Mr. Jennings: Well, Chris asked for help in a pleasant way, so I wanted to help him. I would have liked it if he would have tried to find the answers on his own first, before asking me, but he seemed to really want the help. I got the feeling that he wanted to do the assignment.

Ms. Benson: Thank you very much for helping, Mr. Jennings. All right, did Chris follow Step 1, Steve?

Steve: Yeah.

Ms. Benson: How do you know? What did he do?

Steve: He counted to ten.

Ms. Benson: Good. Did Chris follow Step 2, Bill?

Bill: Yes.

Ms. Benson: How do you know?

Bill: 'Cause he talked it . . . he said what he could do.

Ms. Benson: Did he decide what would be the best choice?

Bill: Yeah. To talk to him and ask him to help.

Ms. Benson: Good. He made a good choice. Step 3, Jenny?

Jenny: Yes. He did it.

Ms. Benson: He made a good choice and then he followed through. Terrific! How do the rest of you think Chris did?

Michelle: He got help.

Tom: Yeah. He did good.

Ms. Benson: Chris, how do you think you did?

Chris:	I did okay.
Ms. Benson:	Would you do anything differently next time?
Chris:	Well, he helped me.
Ms. Benson:	All right, you got the help you needed. And you followed all of the steps to the skill. Did Chris talk to Mr. Gleason in a friendly way?
Jenny:	Yes.
Ms. Benson:	How do you know it was friendly—what did Chris do?
Jenny:	He wasn't mad.
Ms. Benson:	How did Chris look so you know he wasn't mad?
Michelle:	He didn't look like this. (Clenches her teeth and squints.)
Ms. Benson:	Right. His face was relaxed. It wasn't tight and he didn't clench his teeth or make an angry face. What about the rest of his body? Did he make a fist or anything like that?
	(Students say no, shake their heads.)
	What did his voice sound like?
Willie:	He wasn't loud.
Ms. Benson:	Good. Chris, you used your regular speaking voice when you talked to Mr. Gleason. Chris, did you feel angry?
Chris:	No, not after a while.
Ms. Benson:	Did counting to ten give you the time to cool off?
Chris:	Yeah. It really worked.
Ms. Benson:	Chris, you did a very good job following the steps. Is there anything you could do next time to make this even better?
Chris:	Maybe try harder to answer the questions.
Ms. Benson:	You mean to try to do it yourself, before you get angry or ask for help?
Chris:	I guess I should try harder.
Ms. Benson:	That's a good idea to try it on your own, first. But you did a very good job. How did you feel when you acted out the steps?

Chris:	Kinda funny.
Ms. Benson:	Do you mean awkward funny or silly funny?
Chris:	What's awkward?
Ms. Benson:	Like it's not really what you would usually do?
Chris:	Yeah, like that.

(During this time Mr. Jennings is reinforcing the rest of the group for listening to the discussion between Chris and Ms. Benson.)

ASSIGNING HOMEWORK

Ms. Benson:	Chris, when is your next science class?
Chris:	Tomorrow, after P.E. class.
Ms. Benson:	Would you like to give this a try tomorrow?
Chris:	Yeah. I don't want to have to sit in the hall.
Ms. Benson:	(Takes out a Homework 1 sheet.) Chris, you might feel funny doing this skill tomorrow, too, like you felt today. Whenever we do something new, we often feel awkward or a little bit strange. The important thing is to go ahead and just give it a try. Now, Chris, you need to write your name here . . . and put tomorrow's date on the homework sheet, because that's when you'll try out the skill. Chris, who will you try the skill with?
Chris:	Mr. Gleason.
Ms. Benson:	Write his name here. When will you try it?
Chris:	In science.
Ms. Benson:	Good, that goes here.
Chris:	How do you spell science?
Ms. Benson:	S-c-i-e-n-c-e. When we're finished with our group for today, you can write the name of the skill here and the steps to the skill here. You can copy them from the board and I'll help you if you need it. Then, after science tomorrow, when you've tried the skill, you'll tell us what happened—for example, if you had to sit in the hall or not. Okay?
Chris:	Yeah.
Ms. Benson:	Then, where it says How did you do?, you'll circle the happy face if you did a good job—if you followed all the steps. You'll circle this face if you did

	an okay job, like if you forgot one step or you didn't talk in as friendly a way as you could have. Or you'll circle the sad face if you didn't follow the steps. Okay?
Chris:	Yes. If I have to sit in the hall, then I circle a sad face, right?
Mr. Jennings:	No, this is to evaluate only how well you followed the steps. Sometimes you'll do a really great job following the steps, and it still won't work. Hopefully, following the steps will work, like it worked today in the role play. But there will be times, no matter how you try, that the steps won't work. This skill is a plan for you, and, even if you have to sit in the hall, you still circle a happy face if you followed all the steps to the plan.
Chris:	Oh. (As if he understands.)
Ms. Benson:	Try it tomorrow, just like you did today in the role play. Except you can try to answer the questions on your own, first, if that's what you think you should do then. Then, during our group tomorrow afternoon, we'll hear what happened. We'll all be anxious to hear how you did. Do you think you're ready?
Chris:	Yeah!
Mr. Jennings:	For the rest of you, your homework assignment is to come to group tomorrow with a situation you can tell about where you could use the skill of Dealing with Your Anger. It can be a situation that happens at home, with your friends or neighbors, or at school. Chris, you need to copy the name of the skill and the skill steps on your homework sheet. Be sure to take it to science class with you so you can look at the steps if you want to.

ENDING THE SESSION

Mr. Jennings:	Are there any questions?
	(No response)
	Does everyone know what to do for tomorrow?
Michelle:	Yeah, Chris does the skill, and we think of when we need it.
Mr. Jennings:	Right. Any other questions? If not, our time is up, so we'll see all of you tomorrow. Thanks to everyone for listening and joining in today.

SUMMARY

The value of modeling as an aid to learning has been stressed throughout this book, and the illustrative protocol of a Structured Learning session contained in this chapter is intended to be just this type of learning aid. The group leaders' behaviors depict what generally occurs in a Structured Learning session and the students' responses correspond closely to the ways they may actually respond in many sessions. As a further aid to teacher effectiveness, the following chapter provides a variety of suggestions for enhancing the use of Structured Learning.

CHAPTER 8

Suggestions for Use

It is important that teachers and others using Structured Learning feel free to employ their own creativity to enhance the learning process. For example, many skills relevant to the elementary-age child are presented in Chapter 6, but this does not imply that they are the only skills that can or should be taught. Instead, while the Structured Learning components (modeling, role playing, performance feedback, and transfer of training) remain the same, the specific skills, their behavioral steps, and provisions for transfer may be modified from child to child and from group to group. Just as we thus ask the readers to be responsive to their own experience with this method, in the present chapter we wish to share the highlights of our own usage of Structured Learning with skill-deficient children. We will indicate procedures and techniques that seem to clearly enhance the likelihood of successful outcomes.

FLEXIBILITY OF SKILL AGENDA AND CLASSROOM ACTIVITIES

SKILL SHIFTING AND NEW SKILL DEVELOPMENT

Sometimes during instruction in a given prosocial skill, the need may arise for training in a different skill. When the group leader perceives such a circumstance, it is important that she either shift to teaching the new skill on the spot, or make note of the need to do so in a later session. In the illustrative

185

session presented in the preceding chapter, Chris's need for training in another skill became apparent. While being taught Dealing with Your Anger, he seemed to have difficulty in requesting teacher assistance, suggesting the value of instruction for him in Skill 2, Asking for Help. But skilled Structured Learning trainers may need to possess more than the ability to shift in their teaching to different, existing skills. They may also have to build new skills, as their students' skill deficiencies require. Chris's anger and frustration may have derived in part from his inability to approach a class assignment in an organized manner. This skill, Approaching an Assignment, is not an existing Structured Learning skill, and is mentioned here as but one of many possible examples of new skills the perceptive teacher may have to creatively develop.

INTRODUCING NEW SKILLS

To reduce the possible interference of new learning on previously learned materials, a second skill should be introduced only when the student can recall most or all of the steps of the first skill, has had an opportunity to role play it, and has shown some initial transfer outside of the group teaching setting (e.g., a successfully completed homework assignment). When more complicated skills are introduced, 2 to 3 weeks or even longer may be necessary for mastery before proceeding to yet another skill. Periodic review of previously learned skills will reinforce these skills and encourage their use in new situations, provide systematic fading of the teaching to enhance generalization (Buckley & Walker, 1978), and prevent student boredom, which may occur with the concentration on one skill necessary to produce overlearning.

It is also important to note that when students first begin to use prosocial skills on their own (in real-life environments), their performance may be initially somewhat mechanical. This is to be expected. Just as a student who is first learning to read may read words in a labored fashion, students newly employing prosocial behaviors may behave in an awkward or unnatural way. Their performance will occur more naturally with increased practice and real-life reward.

ARRANGING THE CLASSROOM ENVIRONMENT

The classroom teacher might wisely provide opportunities for students to practice the prosocial skills they have learned in the classroom and elsewhere in school. This means, in particular, that within the school day time should be structured to allow students to interact with one another—to talk, work, and play together. Although problems may arise by allowing this type of student-to-student interaction, it also creates unique opportunities for the teacher to guide skill-deficient students in appropriate, prosocial responses. Scheduling free activity or game times, allowing students to work together on academic or content area tasks during specific times of the day, and suggesting that students seek out each other for assistance, rather than asking the teacher for help, are examples of concrete means for stimulating such skill-relevant interaction. Examples of further types of constructive learning activities that provide opportunities for positive peer interaction can also be found in Johnson and Johnson's (1975) material on Cooperative Learning.

INCLUDING STRUCTURED LEARNING
IN THE CURRICULUM

Often it is desirable to include Structured Learning within a school's regular curriculum. Structured Learning is easily integrated into subject areas that deal with personal or interpersonal development such as social studies (e.g., family and community relationships), language arts (e.g., communication skills, problem-solving skills), and health (e.g., dealing with stress, peer relationships). Therefore, a teacher who conducts Structured Learning groups need not feel concerned that she is neglecting instruction in major content areas.

STRATEGIES FOR EFFECTIVE LEARNING

USING BODY LANGUAGE OR BODY TALK

It can be very helpful to skill-deficient students to understand the way their own and others' body and facial expressions convey meaning to the people with whom they interact. Non-verbal communicators (e.g., facial expressions, body posture, hand gestures) can give others messages either consistent with or contradictory to the child's verbal message. Understanding the influence of body language or "body talk" is an important factor in learning prosocial behaviors. Consider, for example, a student who is told to leave the playground for breaking playground rules. Often it is not the breaking of the rule per se that resulted in the playground supervisor's action. Rather, one hears such comments about students as "She was defying my authority" or "He didn't seem sorry for what he did." When the playground supervisor is further questioned regarding the student's defiance or failure to apologize, nonverbal evidence may be called upon, e.g., "She just stood there with her arms crossed and glared" or "He didn't look sorry for what he did." Therefore, students should be made more aware of the ways in which they and others use their bodies and faces to send clear and definite messages.

It is often helpful to list concrete examples of desirable types of body talk as well as negative or undesirable ways to communicate nonverbally (see Table 2 for an example).

A discussion of body talk should optimally be reflected behaviorally in both the modeling and role-playing components of Structured Learning. Additionally, assessment of a child's body language provides an excellent target for performance feedback, helpful to both role player and observers alike.

Table 2. Body Language

FRIENDLY	NOT FRIENDLY
Normal tone of voice	Whiny or loud voice
Smiling	Frowning
Relaxed face	Tight face (teeth clenched)
Hands down to your sides	Hands on hips, arms tightly folded
Standing relaxed	Leaning forward
Hands relaxed	Hands making a fist

ROLE REVERSAL

Role reversal can be a useful technique in Structured Learning, especially with older skill-deficient children. It is particularly helpful when a student's performance anxiety creates difficulty in role playing his own role. The teacher, other group leader, or even a peer can act out the main actor role, while the main actor takes on the role of the person with whom he has the problem. In this case, role reversal assists the student by having another person model the behaviors the student himself needs for dealing with the specific problem. Role reversal may also contribute to the student's empathy or understanding of the antagonist's position. In addition, this technique can be used when more information about the antagonist is needed than that which the student is able to provide verbally. He may be able to imitate the antagonist's manner much better than he can actually describe it.

INSTRUCTED GENERALIZATION

Structured Learning is most effective when it is also integrated into the teacher's behavior management system and the student's instructional and social settings at school. When potential problems arise in the classroom (the teachable moment!), the teacher can elicit a prosocial response from the student by suggesting that the steps to a particular skill be used. This is a positive alternative to reprimanding the student for having the problem, as well as a means for teaching the student when to use a given skill. Each time this happens, the teacher is reminding the student *what to do* rather than *what not to do*. Such an approach turns naturally occurring problem situations into realistic learning opportunities. It provides an environment in which a positive emphasis is placed on learning how to deal with interpersonal problems.

TEACHER MODELING

The teacher, throughout the course of the school day, should model desirable, prosocial behavior, and use the behavioral steps for selected skills when it is appropriate to do so. When

the teacher becomes frustrated or angry with a student's behavior, for example, there is a powerful effect on learning if
the teacher models the steps of Dealing with Your Anger in a
clear and deliberate manner. Needless to say, there also is a
powerful negative effect on students if the teacher models,
instead, a prosocial skill deficiency.

CONTINGENCY CONTRACTING

A contingency contract is an agreement between the teacher
and a student stating a behavioral goal the student will work
to achieve and the reward earned for achieving that goal. The
goal and reward are negotiated by the teacher and student.
Typically, both parties agree to carry out an action—the student to perform a selected behavior (for a given length of
time or a predetermined number of times) and the teacher to
provide the mutually agreed upon reinforcement (e.g., a class
popcorn party).

Homme (1970) presents several rules to follow when implementing contingency contracts. These include the following:

1. Initial contracts should require a small amount of behavior change.
2. The payoff (reward) should be given immediately after
   the performance of the task.
3. Frequent rewards should be provided.
4. Contracts should reward accomplishments rather than
   obedience.
5. The terms should be clearly stated.
6. Contracts should be fair.
7. Contracts should be reviewed regularly.
8. Contracts should be phrased in a positive manner.
9. Contracting should be carried out consistently.

Further, contracts should be in writing, not merely verbal;
signed by both teacher and student; have beginning and ending dates; and, in addition to specifying a particular reward if a
particular behavior change occurs, may also specify a bonus
reward for extraordinary behavior change and a penalty for
absence of any behavior change.

Figure 19 presents a sample contingency contract.* Included in this contract are specifications of the skill to be practiced, the reward to be received when the student meets the behavioral criteria selected, and provisions for contract reevaluation.

FREQUENCY SELF-MONITORING

Frequency self-monitoring is a technique in which students monitor and record their own performance of a selected behavior, in this case, the performance of a selected prosocial skill. Students are given a chart or form on which they record (e.g., color a space, make a tally mark) the number of times they use or practice the selected skill. Kanfer (1975) suggests that several steps be taken when teaching students to record, or monitor, their own behavior. These include the following:

1. Discuss with the student how such monitoring will be helpful (e.g., it will tell both you and me how often you are using the skill on your own).
2. Identify the specific behaviors (what prosocial skill the student will practice and, hence, will record).
3. Select a way to record the student's performance.
4. Show how the student's recording can be graphed (this will show the student her progress).
5. Role play and rehearse the self-monitoring procedure.

We have found this technique to be beneficial for several reasons: (1) The group leader will be able to become aware of the child's functioning in all school settings (i.e., implementing self-monitoring procedures may give the teacher an indication of the frequency with which the student actually attempts the skill); (2) the child's skill performance may not always result in positive reinforcement from others, but recording her performance, to be later shown to the teacher for reinforcement, will let the child know that she will, in fact, be reinforced for these efforts; and (3) many students are far

---

*The *Program Forms* booklet contains a variety of contracts that can be used with students to encourage their practice of the skills learned in the Structured Learning group. It is available from Research Press, P.O. Box 3177, Champaign, IL 61821.

Figure 19. Sample Contingency Contract

I will practice _____

_____
Student

If I do, then _____

_____

_____
Teacher

Date _____

To be reevaluated
on or before

_____
Date

more motivated to use newly learned skills when they, rather than an outside observer, can monitor their own performance.

The majority of students appear to be quite accurate when participating in frequency self-monitoring. However, it may be necessary for the teacher to record some students' performances at the same time that those students record their performances. Comparing the two records should then give an indication of these students' abilities to accurately monitor their skill performances. If a large discrepancy between the recordings is found, students should either be reinstructed in the technique and given another try at self-monitoring, or another system, such as a contingency contract or token system, could be implemented.

Figure 20 presents a sample self-monitoring form.* The skill the child is to monitor is listed on the form, along with a way to mark each time that the skill is performed (e.g., coloring a space, circling a numeral).

EXTERNAL SUPPORT

Of the several principles of transfer of training for which research evidence exists, maximizing real-life reinforcement of skilled behavior is one of the most important. Students will perform the skills they have been taught if there is some "payoff" for doing so. As we have discussed earlier, new behaviors are more likely to endure over time if they are rewarded, but diminish if they are ignored or actively challenged. We have found it useful to implement some supplemental programs outside of the Structured Learning teaching setting that can help to provide more of the rewards students need to maintain their new behaviors.

Prearranged Reinforcement

Because it is critical for students to see that newly learned skills really do work in most situations, the teacher may decide to increase the likelihood of skill use being successful. For instance, in the group described in the preceding chapter, the group leaders may decide to discuss Chris's plan with Mr.

*Additional types of self-monitoring forms are included in the *Program Forms* booklet, available from Research Press, P.O. Box 3177, Champaign, IL 61821.

Figure 20. Sample Self-Monitoring Form

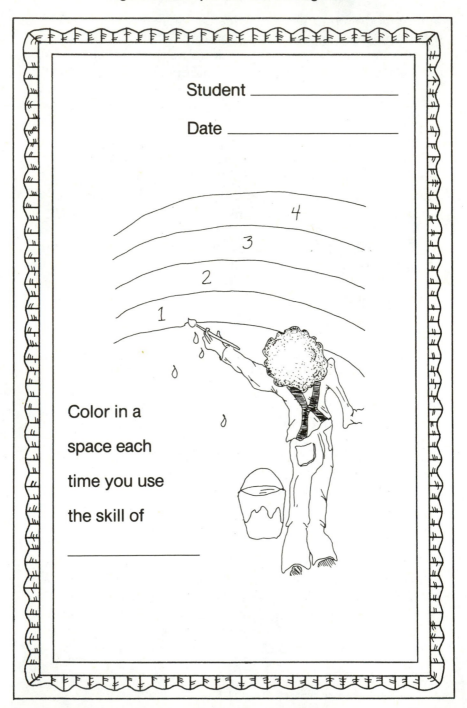

Student _____

Date _____

4

3

2

1

Color in a

space each

time you use

the skill of

_____

Gleason prior to his attempt at the skill. Mr. Gleason could be informed of Chris's desire to do well in his science assignment and the skill steps Chris will try. Specific ways that Mr. Gleason could reinforce Chris if he follows the skill steps could also be suggested. In taking such an action, however, the group leader must consider the receptivity of the person with whom the student will attempt the skill, the student's feelings if he realizes that the teacher was aware of his plan (this may break confidentiality), and the student's competence or chances of succeeding without such a move on the leader's part. This decision must be left to the discretion of each individual group leader.

Orientation Meetings

An additional way of providing environmental support is by holding orientation meetings for school staff and for the families and friends of participating students, i.e., the real-life reward and punishment givers. These meetings acquaint others with Structured Learning, the skills being taught, and the steps that make up these skills. The most important part of these sessions involves presenting ways the school staff, relatives, and friends can encourage and reward children as they practice their new skills. The teachers who instruct the students and school personnel who come into contact with them (e.g., school principal, special class teachers) should in particular be made aware of the specific skills the Structured Learning group or an individual child is seeking to practice. This information sharing should occur on an ongoing basis whenever possible, either verbally or by distribution of a mimeographed note. In addition, encouraging students to share their successfully completed homework assignments with other teachers and school personnel will not only inform others of the skills the students are practicing, but is likely to elicit much needed and deserved words of praise.

Take-Home Skills Journal

To enhance the likelihood that newly learned prosocial behaviors will also be used outside of the instructional setting (e.g., at home), parents should be informed (with the child's permission) of the Structured Learning process and the specific skills their child is being taught. One method of providing ongoing communication with parents is to have each child begin a Take-Home Skills Journal. In order for such a journal to be successful as a means of communication, the classroom teacher must provide for in-class time in which the students will make journal entries.

The Journal is a booklet that can be easily made by creating a construction paper cover and by duplicating Figure 21 to form the pages. Figure 22 presents a sample letter to parents (from the child) that describes how the Journal should be used. (Depending upon the abilities of the students, they may compose a letter, copy one provided on the blackboard, or insert a Xeroxed letter in their Journal.) It can be included as page 1 of the Take-Home Skills Journal. Students should be instructed to take their Journals home, but bring them back to

---

Figure 21. Take-Home Skills Journal

SKILL: _____   (Make your own drawing of
                                     the skill in use.)
STEPS: _____

         _____

         _____

         _____

         _____

         _____   WHEN I PRACTICED! (Make
                                       a happy face or a tally mark.)
         _____

Figure 22. Sample Letter to Parents

We are working on good social skills in our class. Good social skills help us get along better with classmates and adults, help us make friends, and help us handle our feelings. We are learning social skills by deciding on a plan, then we watch people handle problems using this plan. Next we try it out, talk about how we followed the plan, and then we practice it on our own. The skills we practice can be used at school, but we can use them at home, too. On each page of this journal, I'll write the name of the skills and the steps of the plan. Then I'll make a picture to show the skill. This journal will help to remind me to practice the skill when I'm not at school. You can help by suggesting that I practice and by reminding me to mark the times I practice in my journal.

school on a regular basis (such as each day or twice a week). The teacher can then monitor the use of the frequency self-monitoring part of the Journal.

SELF-REWARD

Frequently, environmental support is insufficient to maintain newly learned skills. In fact, many real-life environments in which children live actually resist their efforts at behavior change. It is not uncommon, for example, for skill-deficient children to have peers who consistently reward antisocial, but not prosocial, behavior. For this reason we have found it useful to include the teaching of self-reinforcement procedures.

After a new skill has been taught and the students have made a homework attempt and received feedback on it, we recommend that they continue to practice their new skill as frequently as possible in real-life settings. It is at this time that a program of self-reinforcement can and should be initiated.

First of all, students are taught to evaluate their own performances even if their efforts do not meet with the hoped-for response from others. The students need to know that the skill may not work in all situations, yet they still may deserve to be reinforced for the attempt. For example, if the students follow all of the steps of a particular skill especially well, self-reward might take the form of saying something (e.g., "Good for me" or "I really did that well") and doing something (e.g., "I'll play basketball after school" or "I'll use my allowance for that movie I want to see") as a special reward. Teachers will need to encourage students to provide such self-rewarding statements and privileges by having them rehearse self-reward (e.g., following successful completion of homework assignments or when the teacher has noticed a student using the skill) and assisting them in generating a list of "special activities" that can be rewarding.

USE OF SKILL CUES

Students should be reminded to use the prosocial skills they have practiced in their real-life situations and environments. Classroom teachers can facilitate such use by providing skill cues—reminders that a given prosocial skill could be used. Three types of skill cues are (1) a verbal cue (suggesting that the student try a given skill); (2) cue cards, carried by the student, on which the behavioral steps for a particular skill are written; and (3) cue posters on which the skill steps are displayed in the classroom.

Verbal Cues

When the classroom teacher observes a situation where the use of a prosocial skill is appropriate, the student will be more likely to use the skill if the teacher suggests its use. For example, Todd has completed all of his academic assignments and is sitting quietly at his desk; the teacher then suggests that Todd use the skill of Deciding on Something to Do. The teacher may need to assist Todd further by reviewing the skill steps with him at that time.

Cue Cards

The behavioral steps of a prosocial skill are listed on a 3 x 5-inch cue card, along with a space for the student to check each step, either as she enacts it or after all steps are completed. It is also helpful to include a self-evaluation format, so that the student can evaluate her own skill performance. The student may tape the card to her desk, if it is a skill that is to be used in the classroom, or she may keep it in her pocket or in a folder if it is a skill for use in another setting (e.g., on the school bus, on the playground, in another classroom, or at home). For example, Michelle has trouble staying out of fights on the playground and in the school hallways. Her cue card looks like Figure 23.

Cue Posters

When the group leaders have begun instructing students in a given prosocial skill within the Structured Learning group setting, it will help the students practice the skill if a cue poster is displayed containing the title of the skill and its behavioral steps written on posterboard. The cue poster is placed where it is most appropriate. If students have been instructed in the skill of Playing a Game, for example, displaying a cue poster for this skill in the area of the classroom used for free time activities may remind the students of this particular skill.

Figure 23. Michelle's Cue Card

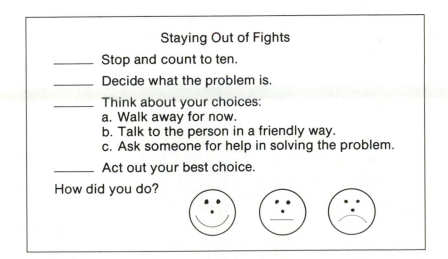

SOCIAL SKILLS GAMES

A variety of games can be developed and used to enhance the learning of social skills. Group games, in and of themselves, require students to practice a variety of social skills (e.g., joining in, sharing, showing sportsmanship, communication skills). Types of games that lend themselves well to Structured Learning include board games and role-play games.

Cartledge and Milburn (1980) make several important points worth considering when using social skills games: (1) The connection between performing a skill in the game setting and in real life needs to be made explicit; (2) the winner should be determined on the basis of performance, rather than solely on the basis of chance; (3) if rewards are used they should be given for appropriate (skilled) participation rather than for winning; (4) participants should not be "out" in a game without provisions for being allowed to participate again within a short period of time; and (5) if teaming is required, skill-deficient children should be included on the same team as skill-competent children.

SKILL OF THE WEEK

One enjoyable activity that enhances the effectiveness of Structured Learning is a Skill of the Week bulletin board. One prosocial skill that has been taught by Structured Learning can be chosen each week. This may be the skill that students are working on at the time or a skill for which review is needed. The class may want to draw pictures of times when they can use the skill and display these along with the title of the skill. Awards may also be given for skill performance (such as the awards presented in Chapter 9) and displayed on the bulletin board. This strategy emphasizes the use of prosocial skills, reminds students to use a selected skill, and provides reinforcement for skill use in a public manner.

PROSOCIAL SKILLS FOLDERS

All students in the Structured Learning group should keep a prosocial skills folder. This is simply a way of organizing the student's materials (e.g., cue cards, homework assignments, contracts, self-monitoring forms, lists of appropriate alternative activities for use with particular skills). Students will then have easy access, when needed, to the behavioral steps to skills they have practiced in the past.

VIDEOTAPING

The use of videotapes can contribute to the effectiveness of Structured Learning in a variety of ways. Modeling displays may be taped and a "library" of effective tapes may thus be collected. Role plays may be taped and used for self-evaluation by allowing participating students to view and reflect upon their own skill performance. Videotapes of Structured Learning sessions may be used (with permission of the participants) to explain its goals and procedures to parents and other potential reward providers. Finally, videotaping the Structured Learning group on a continuing basis may provide a record of the progress that is made by the individual group members over a long period of time.

ADAPTATIONS FOR SPECIAL EDUCATION CLASSES

Our experience indicates that Structured Learning is often particularly beneficial for special education students, but that modifications in the typical use of this method may be necessary. The Structured Learning process must be adapted to the special needs and circumstances of such students.

One modification might include shortening the list of skill steps and simplifying its language for mentally handicapped students. For example, the steps to the skill Listening can be altered to

1. Look.
2. Listen.
3. Ask a question.

Spending more time on each skill (e.g., repeatedly practicing role plays, giving more frequent homework assignments) and providing more frequent reinforcement may also assist in the prosocial skill learning of mentally handicapped students.

The special academic needs of all handicapped students (learning disabled, mentally disabled, and behaviorally disordered) need to be responded to in an analogous manner. For example, the writing of homework assignments should be minimized for students with fine motor difficulties, and students who are unable to read the skill steps should be provided with additional modeling displays and role plays in order to facilitate their memorization of these steps.

ADMINISTRATIVE SUPPORT

When undertaking any new teaching strategy, teachers need the support of their school administrators. Administrators' attitudes toward the value of teaching prosocial behavioral alternatives to students can contribute greatly to the success—or failure—of these teaching efforts. Ideally, administrators will actively support Structured Learning endeavors by providing encouragement and assistance to the teachers or others who are implementing such techniques. Such encouragement and assistance can be given in several ways:

1. Verbally encouraging teachers who are carrying out Structured Learning procedures (i.e., explicitly and publicly stating your belief in its importance).

2. Providing positive reinforcement to these teachers for their teaching efforts (e.g., "I noticed Johnny isn't having as many playground problems since you began Structured Learning; will you share what you are doing at our next staff meeting?").

3. Familiarizing yourself with Structured Learning and offering your direct assistance as a group leader or as a role player or model in one or more Structured Learning groups.

4. Assisting in transfer efforts by suggesting that other teachers implement Structured Learning, by participating in parent and teacher orientation meetings, and by reinforcing the students' use of prosocial skills.

SUMMARY

This chapter presented a variety of suggestions designed to enhance the effectiveness of Structured Learning for prosocial skill acquisition and transfer. The following chapter will discuss a variety of techniques for managing individual and group behavior problems that may occur during Structured Learning instruction.

CHAPTER 9

Managing Behavior Problems

One of the major challenges to the teacher conducting Structured Learning groups is maintaining students' attention and keeping problem behavior under control. Knowledge and careful implementation of management techniques such as those described in this chapter can help. However, it cannot substitute for "good teaching"—that is, the use of the techniques described in Chapter 5—that creates a positive learning environment for skill-deficient children. With this caution in mind, we will describe a variety of management techniques for use with problem behaviors in Structured Learning groups or in mainstream classes.

Once the teacher has identified a management problem, the task becomes one of selecting and implementing one or more techniques designed to foster more appropriate behavior. We do not propose that only certain techniques should be used with certain types of problematic behaviors. Just as one type of reinforcer may be reinforcing for one student but not for another, a particular behavior management strategy is likely to be more effective for one child than for another. Therefore, we will describe a range of management strategies to be used when conducting Structured Learning groups, and urge that Structured Learning teachers seek to individualize their use of these methods, employing those techniques for a given child that appear to work best *with that child.*

Four types of behavior management techniques will be presented. Group I is comprised of instructional techniques developed to assist in the prevention of behavior problems.

Group II contains a variety of surface management techniques, designed to deal with mild behavioral difficulties that occur on an occasional basis, but that have the potential to inhibit the smooth functioning of the group. Group III techniques, behavior modification strategies, are based on those principles of reinforcement that have typically been used to decrease excessive behaviors and to shape infrequently occurring desirable ones. Group IV consists of relationship-based techniques that help to create a supportive atmosphere conducive to learning. These latter techniques are frequently used along with instructional techniques (Group I), surface management techniques (Group II), and behavior modification techniques (Group III).

GROUP I: INSTRUCTIONAL TECHNIQUES

Instructional techniques are designed to prevent any serious behavior problems from developing and to create an environment that will assist the students in making acceptable, prosocial choices regarding their own behavior within the group. This set of techniques includes ones applicable to the total group, described first, as well as ones for use with particular individuals within the group. Several techniques support constructive, task-oriented behavior within the Structured Learning group by providing structure to the learning environment. These structure-enhancing techniques include designing a schedule or routine; defining teacher expectations; providing an encouraging environment; setting limits on student behavior; prompting; and simplification.

DESIGNING A SCHEDULE OR ROUTINE

The teacher should provide a structure for the school day by creating a schedule of events that will take place. Within this schedule, the teacher sets the time for group instruction in Structured Learning and makes provisions for opportunities for students to practice those prosocial skills they have learned in the formal group setting. While most teachers recognize that it is important to have planned events and activities for the students to participate in, informing the students of such a schedule is often overlooked. Yet it can be very productive to begin each school day with a meeting of the entire class, during which time the students can be informed of the activities planned for that day, and their questions or concerns can be answered or discussed. Such a procedure helps avoid many of the problems associated with uncertainty or surprise.

Agenda-setting should also be provided for the Structured Learning sessions themselves. While most students quickly catch on to the pattern of Structured Learning sessions, it is helpful at the beginning of each group meeting to inform the students of the activities that will be taking place (e.g., "We'll be modeling two situations to illustrate the skill of Recognizing Another's Anger, then we'll ask for two volunteers to role play the skill steps," etc.). Letting the students know which activities they will be participating in will help to prepare them for the learning to take place.

DEFINING TEACHER EXPECTATIONS

Familiarizing students with the teacher's expectations for their behavior in the group setting is a crucial aspect of laying a learning foundation. This is most clearly and easily done by establishing group rules. As noted in Chapter 4, students should be encouraged to participate in the development of these rules with as much teacher guidance as needed. If a given behavior valued by the teacher is not generated by this participatory group process, she may add her rule to the list, after explaining the need for it. No more than five or six rules should be established in the beginning stages of instruction, and such rules should be posted in the classroom for easy student reference.

PROVIDING AN ENCOURAGING ENVIRONMENT

The atmosphere of the Structured Learning group, and the classroom as well, should be an encouraging one. By this we mean that the teacher should focus on noticing students following the group rules, making prosocial choices, and "being good," rather than catching them breaking rules or "being bad." While it is impossible to expect any person (teacher or student) to be positive all of the time, a helpful rule to follow is to offer four positive or encouraging statements for each negative statement or reprimand that is given. A benefit of this approach is the observation that when a teacher sees a child behaving appropriately, and states approval of that behavior publicly, students who are engaging in unacceptable behavior are likely to stop the unacceptable behavior and engage in the one that received teacher approval (Kounin, 1977).

One useful way of encouraging students' appropriate behavior while preventing the occurrence of negative behavior is to employ behavioral redirection. Behavioral redirection simply means to engage the student in an appropriate or constructive form of the misbehavior, or in a different type of activity. For example, a student who feels the need to dominate conversation in the Structured Learning group could be requested to dictate his ideas into a tape recorder after the group meeting. Another example of behavioral redirection is to request that a student who brings toys to the Structured Learning group take materials to the office for you and drop her toys off at her locker on the way. This technique thus allows the teacher to emphasize the student's positive, helping actions without having to ignore the student's negative or unconstructive behaviors as well.

SETTING LIMITS ON STUDENT BEHAVIOR

An encouraging focus on the performance of prosocial or acceptable behavior can create a positive learning environment that minimizes serious problematic behaviors. Nevertheless, it is often necessary for the teacher to clarify the limits of his tolerance for given behaviors, and to make these limits known to the students (by telling them). Redl (in Fagen & Hill, 1977) provides guidelines to suggest when limit-setting for given behaviors must be considered.

Protection Against Excitement

The teacher may attend to the situation when the excitement level in an activity is getting out of hand.

During a role play, the actors became extremely silly, and their attitude infected the rest of the group. Although laughter is recognized as important to reduce anxiety in many situations, this situation was clearly out of hand. In order that learning of the skill not be lost, the teacher needed to stop the excitement quickly. He chose to do so by firmly requesting that the role players return to their seats, and another modeling display was carried out.

Protection of an Ongoing Program

The teacher may choose to deal with one child's behavior when this behavior is seriously interrupting the activity for other group members.

EXAMPLE

Michelle began to taunt the other group members. Even though the group leaders provided positive reinforcement to the children who were participating in Structured Learning activities and attempted to proceed with the instruction, Michelle became louder and more disruptive. She was then firmly instructed to leave the group (to take a seat at the side of the classroom) until she felt she could rejoin the group's activities in a constructive manner.

Protection Against Negative Contagion

When one student's behavior is distracting to others, thus interfering with the lesson or activity, and other students are likely to join in the unacceptable behavior, it is appropriate for the teacher to set limits upon the behavior of concern.

EXAMPLE

During the Structured Learning group, Brian removed his baseball cards from his pocket and began distributing them through the group. The group leader firmly requested the cards, put them out of sight, and informed Brian that he could pick up the cards after the session.

Highlighting a Value Area or School Policy

There are times when it is appropriate to deal with a misbehavior by discussing a school policy or a rule related to the misbehavior (e.g., why it is not possible for everyone to be first in line).

EXAMPLE

It was toward the end of the Structured Learning session when several students excitedly requested to role play the skill. The group leader stated that it was possible to role play only one more student's situation that day, because it was near the end of the session. The students' ideas were all written on the chalkboard to serve as a reminder for role-play situations for subsequent Structured Learning sessions. One child was then chosen by the group leader to be the main actor in this day's final role play.

Protecting a Teacher's Inner Comfort

The comfort of the teacher is not the primary factor to consider in setting limits upon problem behaviors, for there are many student behaviors he must learn to be somewhat comfortable with. However, neither should the teacher allow himself to be abused by one or more students.

EXAMPLE

Two students in the Structured Learning group began to complain loudly that the group leaders were unfair—that they only gave the tokens to the students they wanted to. When the students persisted despite being ignored, one leader then stated that she would be willing to discuss their concerns at the end of the session. The students continued with their arguments. The leader then stated: "I said that I would be willing to give you the opportunity to discuss your concerns with me in private. If you choose not to do that, then you must leave the group now."

There also may be other times when a given behavior is clearly unacceptable and needs immediate setting of limits. Such an action might be behavior that is endangering the student or others, the destruction of property, or harassment of a group member by a number of other members.

Setting limits for the behaviors that will be tolerated in the Structured Learning group, informing the students of these limits, and enforcing consequences when the limits are exceeded will further clarify the teacher's behavioral expectations, thus assisting students in acting in acceptable ways and preventing more serious problems from developing.

Other instructional techniques are useful with individual students, rather than the entire class. Prompting and simplification are two such techniques.

PROMPTING

Students practicing a new skill in a Structured Learning session may forget a step or steps, or may have difficulty knowing how to behave in order to carry out a particular step during a role play. The teacher may coach the student on a particular step (give instructional comments or hints to elicit the behavior) or retrain the student in the skill from start to finish.

_____
EXAMPLE
_____

Todd stood up in front of the group to role play the skill of Joining In. He continued to stand there while the two co-actors were playing with Legos. The teacher then said, "Todd, do you recall the first step of Joining In?" Todd shook his head and replied no. The teacher responded: "Decide if you want to join in. Is that what you want to do?" The following dialogue then took place:

Todd:	Yes.
Teacher:	Okay, is this a good time?
Todd:	Yes, because it's free time.

Teacher: Then, what's the next step?

Todd: Decide what to say.

(Todd continues to stand without replying.)

Teacher: Could someone suggest something Todd could say?

Bill: Yeah, you could say, "Could I play, too?"

Michelle: Maybe he could say, "Could I help build the sky-scraper?"

Todd: (Takes a deep breath.) Okay. Guys, could I play with you?

(The two co-actors say "Sure" and "Come on," and Todd begins to help them build with the Legos.)

SIMPLIFICATION

Students' abilities to handle particular group participation tasks will vary. Some may have difficulty following a series of instructions or understanding the meaning of the instructions. For those students, it would be helpful to present fewer instructions at one time or to repeat the instructions, rephrasing them in language that the students can more easily comprehend. In addition, any task may be divided into a sequence of steps that the students can perform one at a time.

Thus, Group I management strategies provide structure to the learning environment and assist students in acting and reacting in a task-oriented manner. Many behavior problems can be controlled or circumvented by the use of these instructional methods.

GROUP II: SURFACE MANAGEMENT TECHNIQUES

Several techniques for managing mild and commonly occurring misbehaviors have been suggested by Redl (in Long & Newman, 1971). These methods, termed "Surface Management" techniques, have been used successfully by us for dealing with problematic behaviors in Structured Learning groups.

PLANNED IGNORING

Many behaviors can be best dealt with by simply ignoring them. Positively reinforcing concurrent appropriate behavior adds to the elimination of the inappropriate action.

EXAMPLE

Behavior: (While two students are participating in a role play, Laura ignores them and, instead, unties and reties her shoelaces again and again.)

Teacher's
Response: Tim and Michelle, thank you for showing the role players that you're interested.

PROXIMITY CONTROL

The teacher physically moves closer to (stands near, sits next to) the student who is misbehaving.

EXAMPLE

Behavior: (While the group is providing feedback to the role players, Tommy begins making throat noises.)

Teacher's
Response: (The teacher quietly leaves her seat in the group, stands next to Tommy, and touches his shoulder while continuing to elicit feedback about the role play.)

SIGNAL INTERFERENCE

These are nonverbal communicators that let the student know her behavior is unacceptable (e.g., eye contact, hand gestures, clearing one's throat, frowning).

EXAMPLE

Behavior: (While the group leaders are modeling the skill, Michelle starts tapping her foot against Tommy's chair. Tommy then hits his foot against Michelle's.)

Teacher's
Response: (While still participating in the modeling, the teacher clears her throat, catches Michelle's eye, and shakes her head back and forth.)

INTEREST BOOSTING

When a child's interest in the group's activity appears to be waning, it is often helpful to redirect the child's interest.

EXAMPLE

Behavior: (Brian was getting restless—moving his chair, turning around—while a student was reporting her performance on a homework assignment.)

Teacher's
Response: Jenny used the skill of Ignoring Distractions during math class. Brian, can you name other classes where Ignoring Distractions might be useful?

TENSION DECONTAMINATION THROUGH HUMOR

A humorous comment can quickly ease a tense situation.

EXAMPLE

Behavior: (While the students were waiting for the teachers to join the Structured Learning group, one of the students drew a picture of the teacher on the blackboard.)

Teacher's
Response: (Looking at the drawing.) Well, that's not such a bad likeness! Except that I think the nose should be a little bit bigger. (She then begins the Structured Learning group.)

RESTRUCTURING THE CLASSROOM PROGRAM

Sometimes the classroom schedule must be abandoned in favor of dealing with a problem that has just occurred. If the class appears tense and upset due to a playground problem, for example, requiring the students to listen to and participate in the skill of Starting a Conversation clearly will not meet their immediate needs. Instead, the teacher should decide to restructure her program.

EXAMPLE

Behavior: (The students came to the Structured Learning group very agitated and loudly complaining that the playground supervisor was unfair in taking a certain disciplinary measure.)

Teacher's
Response: (The teacher requested that each student, one at a time, tell what happened. Allowing the students to discuss the situation brought the level of agitation under control. Then, although the skill of Expressing Affection was the one she had planned to work on, she decided instead to carry out Structured Learning with the more timely skill of Making a Complaint.)

REMOVING SEDUCTIVE OBJECTS

It is natural for students to be distracted by interesting objects and toys. Including the rule of leaving toys and other objects at one's desk may prevent such distractions from occurring during Structured Learning groups.

EXAMPLE

Behavior: (Troy brought a flashlight to the group and began showing it to the group before instruction started.)

Teacher's
Response: Troy, please show everyone your flashlight and how it works. (He does this.) Now, you need to put the flashlight in your desk before we begin. (She points to the rule displayed on the chart.)

DIRECT APPEAL TO VALUES

The teacher appeals to the values of the students (the teacher-student relationship, fairness, reality consequences) in order to stop the misbehavior. The goal is to tell the child that you cannot allow the behavior, but that you still care about him.

EXAMPLE

Behavior: (Troy refused to put his flashlight away.)

Teacher's
Response: Troy, I know that you're proud of your flashlight, but it's one of our rules that you can't have distracting objects when our group begins. It wouldn't be fair to let you break that rule. Let's put it in my desk, then, and that way it will be less likely to get damaged.

ANTISEPTIC BOUNCING

When a child's behavior is not easily controlled, it may be best for the child to "take a break." This is not intended as a punitive measure, but is a strategy for removing the student from a situation before she loses control. With this technique, the student is asked to leave the room to get a drink of water, to run an errand, and so forth.

EXAMPLE

Behavior: (Michelle can't seem to settle down in the group. She continually moves about in her chair and talks to the students sitting next to her.)

Teacher's
Response: (After calling Michelle away from the group.) Michelle, this book needs to go back to the school library and I'd appreciate it if you'd take it for me now. Thanks.

REALITY APPRAISAL

This technique involves giving students an explanation of why a behavior is not acceptable, or "telling it like it is." The approach also assists the students in understanding the consequences of the behavior.

EXAMPLE

Behavior: (During feedback, most of the students began talking all at once.)

Teacher's
Response: If everyone is going to talk at once, we can't hear anyone's ideas.

Group II surface management strategies may be employed for a variety of undesirable student behaviors. There are several advantages to using these techniques. They are relatively unobtrusive, are quickly and easily implemented, and detract little from the actual teaching and learning at the heart of Structured Learning.

GROUP III: BEHAVIOR MODIFICATION TECHNIQUES

Foremost among the behavior modification techniques for dealing with problematic behavior in the classroom is positive reinforcement. Disruptions can be reduced or even eliminated by applying positive reinforcement to class behaviors that should be encouraged, such as attendance, attention, participation (in discussions or role plays), and commitment (evidenced by completing homework assignments, etc.).

Some rules for the use of reinforcement were presented in Chapter 2 (pages 15–18). Some additional ones are relevant here: We will consider the use of social, material, or group reinforcement, shaping, individualized behavior management plans, and extinction techniques.

SOCIAL REINFORCEMENT

Social reinforcement consists of offering praise, approval, or attention to students who exhibit positive classroom behaviors whose frequency we would like to maintain or increase. Research supports the correlation between the use of social reinforcement and an increase in positive behaviors. Becker, Madsen, Arnold, and Thomas (1967) documented the effect of teacher praise on elementary age students; Solomon and Wahler (1973) examined the efficacy of social reinforcement delivered by peers of a group of sixth graders. Goldstein (1983) reviews the research in this area. Examples of social reinforcers are presented in Table 3.

MATERIAL REINFORCEMENT

Material reinforcement consists of concrete rewards for appropriate behavior by students. It is not confined to objects (e.g., food, money, or other prized items), but may be a privilege or activity, or a medium exchangeable for an object or activity at a later date (e.g., tokens). The choice of a material reinforcer should be determined by the child's likes and interests; a particular reinforcer is not equally motivating to all students. Allowing a student to choose a reward from among several creates a more individualized material reinforcement program.

Table 3. Social Reinforcers

NONVERBAL ENCOURAGERS

Smiling	Nearness to the student
Looking interested	Giving a hug
Nodding	Giving a pat on the back
Laughing	Giving applause

VERBAL ENCOURAGERS

Thank you.	You really paid attention.
That's right.	Good thinking.
I'm pleased that you chose to do that.	Good.
	Fantastic.
I like the way you're showing sportsmanship (or other prosocial skill behavior).	Terrific.
	That was a very kind (friendly, caring) thing to do.
Perfect.	Good answer.
Wow!	You did a great job.
I like that.	

Examples of material reinforcers are listed in Table 4. It should be noted that the potency, or reward strength, of many of the activities listed in the table is increased when the activity, in addition to being inherently rewarding, may also bring additional reinforcement from peers and others (e.g., ordering a film, earning extra gym time for the class). A further benefit of certain activity reinforcers (e.g., playing a game with peers, helping the principal) is the degree to which the activity, while serving as a reward, also helps the student practice one or more Structured Learning skills.

We also have developed and made effective use of a type of material reinforcer, given following a student's competent use of particular skills (in role play or in homework), that may best be described as a certificate of achievement award. An example of such an award may be seen in Figure 24.*

As noted earlier, which objects or activities will in fact be reinforcing for a given child will vary from child to child and from time to time. In addition, the strength of selected reinforcers often decreases the more frequently they are used.

---

*Different kinds of award forms appear in the *Program Forms* booklet, which is available from Research Press, P.O. Box 3177, Champaign, IL 61821.

Table 4. Material Reinforcers

OBJECTS

Food (peanuts, raisins, apples, cereal)
Stars/stickers
Pictures to color
Letters of praise to the principal or parents
Ribbons

Pencils, paper, colorful folders
Coupons for McDonald's
"Good Work" buttons
Comic books
Posters
A photograph of the student
Awards

ACTIVITIES

Reading comics
Using the teacher's equipment or materials
Having one-to-one time with the teacher (or principal)
Going early to lunch
Tutoring a younger child
Taking free time in the library
Completing duties for the teacher (e.g., running errands)
Helping in the principal's office
Coloring
Resting
Sharpening pencils
Working with shoes off
Chewing gum
Cooking
Looking through magazines or catalogues
Placing desk anywhere in the room for a work period
Playing with Legos
Listening to a record
Using the tape recorder
Drawing, painting
Taking a 10-minute break
Watering the plants
Taking a Coke break
Completing a task to "beat the timer"
Earning a puzzle piece (completing the puzzle when all pieces are earned)

Earning a piece of a model car (completing the model when all pieces are earned)
Listening to a story on the tape recorder
Using the computer
Dictating a story onto a tape
Using the typewriter
Watching a filmstrip
Doing an assignment on the chalkboard
Playing a game with a friend
Eating lunch in the classroom with a friend
Taking extra recess or gym time with a friend
Bringing a guest to class
Using the telephone
Ordering a film for the entire class
Earning additional recess time (entire class)
Taking a field trip (entire class)
Earning extra gym time (entire class)
Getting early dismissal for lunch (entire class)
Having a class party (e.g., puppet part, Jell-O party, popcorn party)
Having a class break

Figure 24. Sample Certificate of Achievement Award

Classroom Survival Award

to

_____

for using the skill of

_____

Date _____

Thus, some teachers find it useful to create a reinforcement menu (a list of rewards) from which the student can choose. Such a menu may be in the form of an actual list, or be an offer of a combination of tangible rewards and activity rewards in the form of coupons. Each coupon may be a voucher for a particular amount of a given reinforcer (five potato chips, 10 minutes of playing with the gerbil, etc.). Use of a reinforcement menu prevents students from becoming satiated with one reward when it is offered over a period of time and also allows them to determine their own reinforcement choices from several offered.

GROUP REINFORCEMENT

Children are very responsive to the influence of their peers. This phenomenon can be used to encourage the performance of infrequent but desirable behaviors. In using group reinforcement, the teacher provides a reward (e.g., food, activity) to the entire group contingent upon the cooperative behavior of individual group members. Thus, if the reward is meaningful and desirable to the entire group, group members are likely to put pressure on one another to behave appropriately.

EXAMPLE

For the last three sessions, Tammy made statements about how "stupid and dumb" she thought the Structured Learning group was. When Tammy made these remarks, other students joined in by adding their derogatory comments. The group leaders decided to deal with this problem by telling the students that if, for the next three Structured Learning sessions, they encouraged each other's participation in the Structured Learning activities, they would have a popcorn party and watch one of their favorite films. The teacher prepared a small chart on which she wrote the dates of the next three sessions and a space for marking how frequently encouraging statements were offered. The party was a desirable enough group reinforcer that when Michelle began her usual comments the other students began to insist that she stop disrupting the group.

SHAPING

The first time a student practices an unfamiliar behavior, her performance of it may be rough or imperfect. This is true for classroom behaviors such as participating or paying attention, which may not have been exhibited often by a particular student. Therefore, even a partial or flawed performance should be reinforced in early sessions. As the student becomes more confident and skilled in performing the behavior, rewards are given for the improved skill behaviors, and eliminated for the earlier and less adequate approximations. Gradually, the rewarded performance will come to approximate the target behavior. The student's performance is thus "shaped" by the teacher. Social behavior can be shaped according to the following guidelines, developed by Sloane (1976).

1. Find some behavior in which the child is currently engaging that is a better approximation of your goal for him than his usual behavior and reinforce this approximation each time it occurs.
2. When an approximation has become more frequent for several days, select a slightly better one for reinforcement and stop reinforcing the first.
3. Each approximation should be only slightly different from the last one.
4. Let a new approximation receive many reinforcements before moving on to another approximation.
5. Never look a gift horse in the mouth, but reinforce any behavior that is better than that currently required. (pp. 68–70)

EXAMPLE

Brian frequently became upset when moving his chair to sit with the group during the Structured Learning session. He claimed that other students did not quickly move their chairs to make a space for him. He often shouted at them to move, stomped on their feet with his foot, or complained to the teacher. Thus, the Structured Learning group leaders decided to teach the skill of Asking a Favor. Following instruction with this skill, Brian was prompted to use the skill when joining the Structured Learning group. Initially, Brian asked his favor by saying "Would you move? I want to sit here." For this,

Brian received praise from the teacher, because this request was considerably more acceptable than his past behavior. Brian also received additional reinforcement—the students moved their chairs to accommodate Brian. However, Brian's request could have been a much more pleasant one. He again role played the skill of Asking a Favor, and was reinforced only when his request became more and more appropriate ("Could you please make room for me?").

INDIVIDUALIZED BEHAVIOR MANAGEMENT PLANS

At times, a more systematic, structured behavior management plan is needed to create the desired change in problematic behaviors for individual students. The following is a step-by-step system to develop such a plan.

Step 1: Identify the target behavior to be changed. To do this, first list the student's problematic behaviors. Then choose one behavior to decrease in frequency (e.g., the one that bothers you as the teacher the most; the one that would be the easiest to decrease the frequency of; the one that is creating the greatest problem for the student).

Step 2: Decide on the positive behavior that is incompatible with the undesirable behavior. For example:

UNDESIRABLE BEHAVIOR	DESIRABLE OR PROSOCIAL BEHAVIOR
Off-task	On-task
Shouting out	Appropriate request for help
Watching whatever is going on	Ignoring distractions
Running around the room	Following instructions or staying in seat
Sitting alone on the playground	Playing with others on the playground

Step 3: Take baseline data (How frequently does the behavior of concern occur? How frequently does the incompatible behavior occur?) to determine whether or not the prescribed intervention is actually decreasing the behavior of concern. This process need not be a complicated one. For example, the teacher may list the undesirable behavior and the incompatible behavior and make a tally mark for each occurrence of the

behavior on a given day. Accurate baseline information can be obtained in 3 to 5 observation days. For example:

DAYS OBSERVED	BEHAVIOR OF CONCERN	INCOMPATIBLE BEHAVIOR
	Shouting out	Appropriate request for help
Monday		
Tuesday		
Wednesday		
Thursday		

Step 4: Determine the reinforcer: *Watch* for the activities the student seems to particularly enjoy, and *listen* to the student. Ask him what he would like to work for or what activities he particularly enjoys. Consult the previous sections on types of reinforcers (social, material, group) for suggestions of reinforcers that may be offered.

Step 5: Determine the frequency of reinforcement delivery. If the reward is given immediately following the performance of the desirable behavior, it is more likely that the behavior will be repeated. Consequently, some type of small reinforcement (e.g., verbal encouragement, token, point) should be given immediately following the behavior the teacher wants to increase. It should also be decided when the larger reinforcements (e.g., class party, or time to play a game or engage in a desired activity) should be given. Some students may need an activity or privilege several times a day, while for some, large rewards given at the end of the day or week will be sufficient to increase the frequency of the desired behavior. As noted earlier, when first learning a new skill, some type of reward should be provided for every occurrence of the behavior, whenever possible. This reinforcement schedule can then gradually be thinned to an occasional or intermittent schedule.

Step 6: Tracking behavior change. By means of both self-monitoring (pages 191–193) and behavioral observation (pages 27–28) procedures, both the student and teacher will optimally gather ongoing information on the degree to which desired behavioral changes are in fact occurring.

Figure 25 provides a summary of steps in developing an individualized behavior management plan. Following the determination of the target behavior to be changed or decreased, the frequency at which the behavior occurs, the desirable behavior to be increased, and the specific reinforcer and frequency of reinforcement needed by the particular student, the teacher is fully prepared to alter problematic behaviors.

EXTINCTION

The principle of extinction is the obverse of that of reinforcement. Extinction involves the withholding or withdrawal of reinforcement for the performance of previously reinforced behaviors. If behaviors do not meet with reward, they will gradually decrease in frequency, intensity, or duration because

---

Figure 25. Individualized Behavior Management Plan

Step 1. Identify the target behavior to be changed.
   A. List the student's problematic behaviors:

   _____

   _____

   _____

   _____

   B. Choose the target behavior.

   _____

Step 2. Decide on the desirable incompatible behavior.

   _____

Step 3. Obtain baseline frequency data.
   A. Number of days observed _____
   B. Average daily occurrence of behavior of concern

   _____

   C. Average daily occurrence of incompatible behavior

   _____

Step 4. List the reinforcers desired by the student.

   _____

   _____

   _____

   _____

Step 5. Decide how frequently a reward will be given.

   _____

Step 6. Track the behavior change that has occurred.

there is no longer any motivating factor for their performance. This technique is particularly applicable to disruptive behaviors that were reinforced by teacher attention and peer amusement or approval.

EXAMPLE

Ray joined the Structured Learning group quite upset about getting caught cheating on a test. He began mumbling under his breath and continued this behavior to the point of creating a distraction for the other group members. The group was reminded of the skill Ignoring Distractions. The group was also told that Ray was upset and it would be best if he were left alone for now.

One note of caution is in order: Before a response extinguishes, it may temporarily increase in frequency (the extinction burst). This effect may be viewed as an attempt by the student to maintain previous levels of reinforcement for the behavior. Since each performance of the behavior results in so little reinforcement, the student feels that he must engage in the behavior more often or more extremely to get the amount of attention (or other reinforcer) that is desired.

EXAMPLE

Brian had been gaining attention by talking in a high-pitched, whiny voice and making animal noises. The teacher had talked with the group about ignoring Brian's noises and encouraged them to look at Brian and answer his questions only when he spoke in his "regular" voice. However, Brian's noises continued to get louder and more frequent, and several students complained. The teacher encouraged the other students to continue ignoring Brian's noises by saying that if he continued to receive attention for these noises, he would continue to make them. The teacher then began to give praise to the group members who did ignore Brian's noises.

Time out is one type of extinction technique that is frequently useful. This technique involves removing the student from positive reinforcement (e.g., attention) when other forms of extinction (i.e., Planned Ignoring) do not work. This procedure should only be implemented when students have been forewarned of the specific behaviors that will warrant its use and when other management techniques have failed. Time out should be used only as a last resort, for it not only removes the student from positive reinforcement, it also removes him from exposure to the learning environment.

Most often time out involves removing the disruptive student from the classroom to a quiet place where stimulation is minimized (i.e., without other people or distractions). An alternative to actual removal from the class is to place the student in a "time out condition" (Givner & Graubard, 1974) while remaining in the classroom. In such an instance, the disruptive student is prevented from interacting with others in the classroom by instructing classmates to ignore him. The disruptive student may be requested to remove himself from the group (e.g., into another part of the classroom). This form of time out has the important advantage over classroom removal that it still allows the student to learn from the teaching being conducted while removing him from receiving positive reinforcement for undesirable behaviors. The student may be allowed to return to active participation in the group when the time-out time span has been reached, or, as some users of time out suggest, as soon as he feels he is ready to return. When the student does return to the instructional setting, it is critical that he receive positive reinforcement immediately for any type of appropriate behavior. The teacher must create an environment where the student wants to be, or time out itself may, in fact, be seen by the student as a positive alternative.

EXAMPLE

Ray entered the Structured Learning session very angry and began tapping students on their heads with his pencil. Several students shouted at Ray to stop. The teacher requested that the students move away from Ray and try to ignore him. She also requested that Ray take a note to the teacher down the hall (antiseptic bouncing). Ray refused this request as well as the subsequent attempts the teacher made to talk with Ray aside from the other students. Instead, Ray began to poke others with his pencil. The students had been informed in the previous session that those who participated in an active disruption that prevented the group's activities from taking place might be removed from the group. Therefore, the teacher said, "Ray, one of our rules is that anyone who keeps the class from doing its work will not be allowed to be a part of the group. According to this rule, you must leave the group for now. You may take a seat at the side of the room, and when you are ready to cooperate in what we are doing, we'd like to have you back in the group."

GROUP IV: RELATIONSHIP-BASED TECHNIQUES

Psychologists and educators have long known that the better the relationship between the helper and client or student, the more positive and productive the outcome of their interaction is likely to be. In fact, some would hold that the establishment and maintenance of a positive relationship is the most potent factor in effecting behavior change in the student. We take the position that a positive relationship between the teacher and student in a Structured Learning group is a valuable tool that the teacher should utilize in order to effect desired behavior within the group. There are a number of specific techniques that draw primarily upon the relationship between teacher and student. One such technique, Providing an Encouraging Environment, was described earlier, along with the other structure-setting Instructional Techniques. As also mentioned earlier, these various relationship-based techniques can often be combined with other classroom management techniques for maximum effect.

EMPATHIC ENCOURAGEMENT

Using this technique, the teacher first shows the student that she understands the difficulty the student is experiencing, and then urges the student to participate as instructed. This technique consists of the following series of steps:

1. The teacher offers the student the opportunity to explain in detail his difficulty in participating as instructed and listens nondefensively.

2. The teacher expresses an understanding of the student's feelings and behavior.
3. If appropriate, the teacher responds that the student's view is a viable alternative.
4. The teacher restates her view with supporting reasons and probable outcomes.
5. The teacher expresses the appropriateness of delaying a resolution of the problem.
6. The teacher urges the student to tentatively try to participate.

EXAMPLE

While two students were role playing the skill of Responding to Teasing, Michelle leaned back in her chair and began to sneer in an angry manner. The group leader quickly gave positive reinforcement (praise) to those who were attending to the role play and who were successful in ignoring Michelle's behavior. After several minutes of ignoring Michelle, waiting for her behavior to extinguish, the leader noticed that Michelle became even more restless and began muttering loudly enough to be quite distracting to the group. While one leader began to lead the group in providing feedback to the role players, the other leader requested that Michelle talk with him away from the group.

The leader began by saying "Michelle, you appear quite angry. What's the problem?" Michelle responded by stating that it was stupid to ignore someone who was teasing her, because they wouldn't stop. The only thing that would get the kids to stop teasing was to beat them up. The teacher expressed his understanding of how horrible it can feel to be teased, but that fighting seems to result in getting physically hurt and getting into trouble as well. "Sometimes kids tease so that they can get someone into trouble. Our goal is to deal with teasing in a way where you won't get hurt and you'll also stay out of trouble." Michelle stood quietly without speaking. "Michelle, did you want to say something?" (No response.) "Well, let's not decide if this is a useful skill for you until you try it out in a role play. Is that reasonable?" Michelle replied that that was okay, and she and the teacher rejoined the group.

THREAT REDUCTION

Students may find role playing or other types of participation in Structured Learning sessions to be anxiety-provoking or threatening, and may react with inappropriate or disruptive behaviors, or withdraw. To prevent this problem, the teacher should create a supportive environment in which students need not be embarrassed to try practicing new skills at which they may be clumsy. The teacher should provide reassurance or even physical contact (a hand on the student's shoulder, a hug, etc.). The teacher should also encourage the group to express its support of role-play volunteers and others who participate. Shaping of skills allays students' fears by providing them with success and encouragement even in the early stages of learning a skill (Gardner, 1974).

EXAMPLE

Todd was the last to role play in the Structured Learning group. He had declined several earlier invitations to do so, and thus far the group leaders had responded only by encouraging him to participate in giving feedback to other role players. The group leaders felt that threat reduction in the form of offering supportive reassurance and physical closeness would be useful. One group leader called Todd's name and said, "Todd, I'd like you to come up here and together we'll start the role play for the skill of Joining In. I know it's not easy the first time, so let's start it together." She put her arm around Todd's shoulder. "Let's think of some situations in which Todd could use the skill of Joining In and, Todd, then you can choose one of these situations to role play."

DEALING WITH SPECIFIC, COMMON PROBLEMS

We have offered a variety of techniques to assist the Structured Learning group leaders in managing effective group instruction. As stated at the beginning of this chapter, no one technique used for a particular behavior problem will be effective for all students. With this in mind, we have provided a list of the major behavior management problems that commonly occur in Structured Learning groups with elementary-age children and the management techniques that may be employed with each problem. These suggestions are presented in addition to the instructional techniques (Group I) previously described, which are in fact vital to the success of any Structured Learning group.

Disruptive Behavior
Planned Ignoring (Group II)
Proximity Control (Group II)
Signal Interference (Group II)
Interest Boosting (Group II)
Direct Appeal to Values (Group II)
Antiseptic Bouncing (Group II)
Reality Appraisal (Group II)
Social/Material Reinforcement for participating (Group III)
Group Reinforcement (Group III)
Extinction/Time out (Group III)
Empathic Encouragement (Group IV)

Distractibility
Proximity Control (Group II)
Signal Interference (Group II)
Interest Boosting (Group II)
Removing Seductive Objects (Group II)
Social/Material Reinforcement for participating (Group III)
Extinction (Group III)

Aggressive Behavior
Social/Material Reinforcement for nonaggressive behavior
   (Group III)
Contingency Contracting for use of prosocial skill (Group III)
Frequency Self-monitoring plan for use of prosocial skill (Group III)
Time out (Group III)
Empathic Encouragement (Group IV)

Tardiness
Reality Appraisal (Group II)
Social/Material Reinforcement for being on time (Group III)
Group Reinforcement (Group III)
Contingency Contracting for being on time (Group III)
Frequency Self-monitoring for being on time (Group III)

Threats to Quit Group
Social/Material Reinforcement for participating (Group III)
Contingency Contracting for attendance (Group III)
Frequency Self-monitoring for attendance (Group III)
Extinction (Group III)
Empathic Encouragement (Group IV)

Anxiety/Upset

Prompting, Simplification (Group I)
Tension Decontamination through Humor (Group II)
Restructuring the Classroom Program (Group II)
Antiseptic Bouncing (Group II)
Shaping (Group III)
Empathic Encouragement (Group IV)
Threat Reduction (Group IV)

"I Don't Care" Behavior

Interest Boosting (Group II)
Social/Material Reinforcement for participating (Group III)
Group Reinforcement (Group III)
Contingency Contracting for participation (Group III)
Empathic Encouragement (Group IV)

Withdrawal

Prompting, Simplification (Group I)
Interest Boosting (Group II)
Social/Material Reinforcement for participating (Group III)
Empathic Encouragement (Group IV)
Threat Reduction (Group IV)

Walking Out

Social/Material Reinforcement for participating (Group III)
Group Reinforcement (Group III)
Contingency Contracting for participating (Group III)
Extinction (Group III)

Active Refusal to Participate

Prompting (Group I)
Interest Boosting (Group II)
Social/Material Reinforcement for participating (Group III)
Group Reinforcement (Group III)
Empathic Encouragement (Group IV)

Failure to Complete Homework Assignments

Social/Material Reinforcement for homework completion (Group III)
Contingency Contracting for homework completion (Group III)
Frequency Self-monitoring plan for homework completion (Group III)
Empathic Encouragement (Group IV)
Threat Reduction (Group IV)

SUMMARY

Problematic behaviors in a Structured Learning group are those
behaviors that interfere with or detract from the group's process as an active, facilitative learning environment. We have

categorized these behaviors broadly as excessive and deficient, and have described a variety of techniques for dealing with specific types of excesses or deficiencies. Instructional techniques, surface management techniques, behavior modification techniques, and relationship-based techniques have been presented. All of these techniques share the common goal of helping the skill-deficient child become actively involved in Structured Learning groups so that the skills being taught can be learned and practiced effectively.

Reference Notes

1. Rathjen, D., Hiniker, A., & Rathjen, E. *Incorporation of behavioral techniques in a game format to teach children social skills.* Paper presented at the meeting of the Association for Advancement of Behavior Therapy, New York, 1976.

2. Wood, R., Michelson, L., & Flynn, J. *Assessment of assertive behavior in elementary school children.* Paper presented at the meeting of the Association for Advancement of Behavior Therapy, Philadelphia, 1978.

3. Greenwood, C., Walker, H., Todd, N., & Hops, H. *Description of withdrawn children's behavior in pre-school settings* (Report No. 40). Eugene, Oreg.: Center at Oregon for Research in the Behavioral Education of the Handicapped, University of Oregon, 1978.

4. Hawkins, W. *The red flag technique.* Paper presented at the Third Annual Midwest Conference on Behavioral Disorders, Ames, Iowa, 1980.

References

Allen, K. E., Benning, P. M., & Drummond, T. W. Integration of normal and handicapped children in a behavior modification preschool: A case study. In G. Semb (Ed.), *Behavior analysis and education.* Lawrence, Kans.: University of Kansas Press, 1972.

Arbuthnot, J. Modification of moral judgment through role-playing. *Developmental Psychology,* 1975, *11,* 319–324.

Bandura, A. *Social learning theory.* Englewood Cliffs, N.J.: Prentice-Hall, 1977.

Bandura, A., Ross, D., & Ross, S. A. Transmission of aggression through imitation of aggressive models. *Journal of Abnormal and Social Psychology,* 1961, *63,* 575–582.

Barclay, J. Interest patterns associated with measures of desirability. *Personality Guidance Journal,* 1966, *45,* 56–60.

Becker, W. C., Madsen, C. H., Arnold, C. R., & Thomas, D. R. The contingent use of teacher attention and praising in reducing classroom behavior problems. *Journal of Special Education,* 1967, *1,* 287–307.

Bernstein, D. A., & Borkovec, T. D. *Progressive relaxation training.* Champaign, Ill.: Research Press, 1973.

Bornstein, P. H., & Quevillon, R. P. The effects of a self-instructional package on overactive preschool boys. *Journal of Applied Behavior Analysis,* 1976, *9,* 179–188.

Bryan, T. S., & Bryan, J. H. Social interactions of learning disabled children. *Learning Disabilities Quarterly,* 1978, *1,* 33–38.

Bryan, T. S., Wheeler, R., Felcan, J., & Henek, T. "Come on dummy": An observational study of children's communication. *Journal of Learning Disabilities,* 1976, *9,* 53–61.

Buckley, N. K., & Walker, H. M. *Modifying classroom behavior: A manual of procedures for classroom teachers* (Rev. ed.). Champaign, Ill.: Research Press, 1978.

Callantine, M. F., & Warren, L. M. Learning sets in human concept formation. *Psychological Reports,* 1955, *1,* 363–367.

Camp, B. W., & Bash, M. A. *Think aloud: Increasing social and cognitive skills—A problem-solving program for children* (Primary Level). Champaign, Ill.: Research Press, 1981.

Canale, J. R. The effects of modeling and length of ownership on sharing behavior of children. *Social Behavior and Personality,* 1977, *5,* 187–191.

Cartledge, G., & Milburn, J. F. *Teaching social skills to children.* New York: Pergamon Press, 1980.

Chesler, M., & Fox, R. *Role playing methods in the classroom.* Chicago: Science Research Associates, 1966.

Cowen, E. L., Pederson, A., Babigian, H., Izzo, L. D., & Trost, M. A. Long-term follow-up of early detected vulnerable children. *Journal of Consulting and Clinical Psychology,* 1973, *41,* 438–446.

Cox, R. D., & Gunn, W. B. Interpersonal skills in the schools: Assessment and curriculum development. In D. P. Rathjen & J. P. Foreyt (Eds.), *Social competence: Interventions for children and adults.* New York: Pergamon Press, 1980.

Davis, K., & Jones, E. E. Changes in interpersonal perception as a means of reducing cognitive dissonance. *Journal of Abnormal and Social Psychology,* 1960, *61,* 402–410.

Deluty, R. H. Children's action tendency scale: A self-report measure of aggressiveness, assertiveness and submissiveness in children. *Journal of Consulting and Clinical Psychology,* 1979, *47,* 1061–1071.

Duncan, C. P. Transfer after training with single versus multiple tasks. *Journal of Experimental Psychology,* 1958, *55,* 63–73.

Evers, W. L., & Schwarz, J. C. Modifying social withdrawal in preschoolers: The effects of filmed modeling and teacher praise. *Journal of Abnormal Psychology,* 1973, *1,* 248–256.

Fagen, S. A., & Hill, J. M. *Behavior management: A competency-based manual for in-service training.* Washington, D.C.: Psychoeducational Resources, 1977.

Fairchild, L., & Erwin, W. M. Physical punishment by parent figures as a model of aggressive behavior in children. *Journal of Genetic Psychology,* 1977, *130,* 279–284.

Federal Register, Public Law 94-142, Education for All Handicapped Children Act of 1975.

Fitzgerald, G. E. The use of objective observational data in the identification of emotionally disabled pupils. In C. R. Smith & J. Grimes (Eds.), *The identification of emotionally disabled pupils: Data and decision making.* Des Moines, Iowa: Iowa Department of Public Instruction, 1979.

Friedenberg, W. P. *Verbal and non-verbal attraction modeling in an initial therapy interview analogue.* Unpublished master's thesis, Syracuse University, 1971.

Gardner, W. J. *Children with learning and behavior problems: A behavior management approach.* Boston: Allyn and Bacon, 1974.

Givner, A., & Graubard, P. S. *A handbook of behavior modification for the classroom.* New York: Holt, Rinehart & Winston, 1974.

Goldstein, A. P. *Structured Learning Therapy: Toward a psychotherapy for the poor.* New York: Academic Press, 1973.

Goldstein, A. P. *Psychological skill training.* New York: Pergamon Press, 1981.

Goldstein, A. P. Behavior modification approaches to aggression prevention and control. In Center for Research on Aggression (Ed.), *Prevention and control of aggression.* New York: Pergamon Press, 1983.

Goldstein, A. P., Heller, K., & Sechrest, L. B. *Psychotherapy and the psychology of behavior change.* New York: Wiley, 1966.

Goldstein, A. P., Sprafkin, R. P., & Gershaw, N. J. *Skill training for community living: Applying Structured Learning Therapy.* New York: Pergamon Press, 1976.

Goldstein, A. P., Sprafkin, R. P., Gershaw, N. J., & Klein, P. *Skillstreaming the adolescent.* Champaign, Ill.: Research Press, 1980.

Greenwood, C., Walker H., & Hops, H. Issues in social interaction/withdrawal assessment. *Exceptional Children,* 1977, *43,* 490–499.

Gresham, F. M. Assessment of children's social skills. *Journal of School Psychology,* 1981, *19,* 120–133.

Gronlund, H., & Anderson, L. Personality characteristics of socially accepted, socially neglected and socially rejected junior high school pupils. In J. Seiderman (Ed.), *Educating for mental health.* New York: Crowell, 1963.

Grusec, J. E., Kuczynski, L., Rushton, J. P., & Simutis, Z. M. Modeling, direct instruction and attributions: Effects on altruism. *Developmental Psychology,* 1978, *14,* 51–57.

Homme, L. *How to use contingency contracting in the classroom.* Champaign, Ill.: Research Press, 1970.

Hops, H., Fleischman, D. H., Guild, J., Paine, S., Street, A., Walker, H. M., & Greenwood, C. R. *Program for establishing effective relationship skills (PEERS): Consultant manual.* Eugene, Oreg.: Center at Oregon for Research in the Behavioral Education of the Handicapped, University of Oregon, 1978.

Hubbel, A. Two person role-playing for guidance in social readjustment. *Group Psychotherapy,* 1954, *7,* 249–254.

Iannotti, R. J. Effect of role-taking experiences on role taking, empathy, altruism and aggression. *Developmental Psychology,* 1977, *13,* 274–281.

Johnson, D. W., & Johnson, R. T. *Learning together and alone: Cooperation, competition and individualization.* Englewood Cliffs, N.J.: Prentice-Hall, 1975.

Kanfer, F. H. Self-management methods. In F. H. Kanfer & A. P. Goldstein (Eds.), *Helping people change.* New York: Pergamon Press, 1975.

Kaufman, J. M., Gordon, M. E., & Baker, A. Being imitated: Persistence of an effect. *Journal of Genetic Psychology,* 1978, *132,* 319–320.

Kirkland, K. D., & Thelen, M. H. Uses of modeling in child treatment. In B. B. Lahey & A. E. Kazdin (Eds.), *Advances in clinical child psychology.* New York: Plenum Press, 1977.

Kleinsasser, L. D. *The reduction of performance anxiety as a function of desensitization, pre-therapy vicarious learning, and vicarious learning alone.* Unpublished doctoral dissertation, Pennsylvania State University, 1968.

Koegel, R. L., & Rincover, A. Treatment of psychotic children in a classroom environment: I. Learning in a large group. *Journal of Applied Behavior Analysis,* 1977, *7,* 45–59.

Kounin, J. *Discipline and group management in classrooms.* Huntington, N.Y.: Krieger Publishing, 1977.

Kounin, J., & Obradovic, S. Managing emotionally disturbed children in regular classrooms: A replication and extension. In N. J. Long, W. C. Morse, & R. G. Newman (Eds.), *Conflict in the classroom: The education of emotionally disturbed children.* Belmont, Calif.: Wadsworth, 1971.

Larrivee, B. Effective teaching behaviors for mainstreaming. *The Pointer,* 1981, *25,* 28–30.

Lichtenstein, E., Keutzer, C. S., & Himes, K. H. Emotional role-playing and changes in smoking attitudes and behaviors. *Psychological Reports,* 1969, *23,* 379–387.

Long, N. J., & Newman, R. G. Managing surface behavior of children in school. In N. J. Long, W. C. Morse, & R. G. Newman (Eds.), *Conflict in the classroom: The education of emotionally disturbed children.* Belmont, Calif.: Wadsworth, 1971.

Lowe, M. L., & Cuvo, A. J. Teaching coin summation to the mentally retarded. *Journal of Applied Behavior Analysis,* 1976, *9,* 483–489.

Mann, J. H. Experimental evaluations of role-playing. *Psychological Bulletin,* 1956, *53,* 227–234.

Mann, R. A. Assessment of behavioral excesses in children. In M. Hersen & A. S. Bellack (Eds.), *Behavioral assessment: A practical handbook.* New York: Pergamon Press, 1972.

Marlatt, G. A., Jacobson, E. A., Johnson, D. L., & Morrice, D. J. Effect of exposure to a model receiving evaluative feedback upon subsequent behavior in an interview. *Journal of Consulting and Clinical Psychology,* 1970, *34,* 194–212.

Mately, R. E., & Acksen, B. A. The effect of role playing discrepant positions on change in moral judgments and attitudes. *Journal of Genetic Psychology,* 1976, *128,* 189–200.

McGehee, N., & Thayer, P. W. *Training in business and industry.* New York: Wiley, 1961.

McGinnis, E., Sauerbry, L., & Nichols, P. Teaching social skills: A "skillstreaming" plan for elementary-age behaviorally disordered children. *Teaching Exceptional Children,* in press.

Meichenbaum, D., & Cameron, R. Stress inoculation training: Toward a general paradigm for training coping skills. In D. Meichenbaum & M. E. Jarembo (Eds.), *Stress reduction and prevention.* New York: Plenum Press, 1983.

Mesibov, G. B., & LaGreca, A. M. A social skills instructional module. *The Directive Teacher,* 1981, *3,* 6–7.

Morse, W. C. A place for affective education in special education. *Teaching Exceptional Children,* 1982, *15,* 209–211.

Nichols, H. Role-playing in primary grades. *Group Psychotherapy,* 1954, *7,* 238–241.

O'Leary, K. D., & Johnson, S. B. Psychological assessment. In H. C. Quay & J. Werry (Eds.), *Psychopathological disorders of childhood.* New York: Wiley, 1979.

Patterson, G. R., Reid, J. G., Jones, R. R., & Conger, R. E. *A social learning approach to family intervention.* Eugene, Oreg.: Catalia, 1975.

Perry, M. A. *Didactic instructions for and modeling of empathy.* Unpublished doctoral dissertation, Syracuse University, 1970.

Quay, H. C. Classification. In H. C. Quay & J. Werry (Eds.), *Psychopathological disorders of childhood.* New York: Wiley, 1979.

Quay, H. C., & Peterson, D. R. *Manual for the behavior problem checklist.* Champaign, Ill.: Children's Research Center, University of Illnois, 1967.

Rathjen, D. P. An overview of social competence. In D. P. Rathjen & J. P. Foreyt (Eds.), *Social competence: Interventions for children and adults.* New York: Pergamon Press, 1980.

Roff, M., Sells, S. B., & Golden, M. *Social adjustment and personality development in children.* Minneapolis: University of Minnesota Press, 1972.

Rogers-Warren, A., & Baer, D. M. Correspondence between saying and doing: Teaching children to share and praise. *Journal of Applied Behavior Analysis,* 1976, *9,* 335–354.

Rosenthal, T. L. Modeling therapies. In M. Hersen, R. M. Eisler, & P. M. Miller (Eds.), *Progress in behavior modification* (Vol. 2). New York: American Press, 1976.

Ross, D. M., Ross, S. A., & Evans, T. A. The modification of extreme social withdrawal by modeling with guided participation. *Journal of Behavior Therapy and Experimental Psychiatry,* 1976, *2,* 273–279.

Shoabs, N. E. Role playing in the individual psychotherapy interview. *Journal of Individual Psychology,* 1964, *26,* 84–89.

Shore, E., & Sechrest, L. Concept attainment as a function of number of positive instances presented. *Journal of Educational Psychology,* 1961, *52,* 303–307.

Sloane, H. N. *Classroom management: Remediation and prevention.* New York: Wiley, 1976.

Solomon, R. W., & Wahler, R. G. Peer reinforcement control of classroom problem behavior. *Journal of Applied Behavior Analysis,* 1973, *6,* 49–56.

Spivack, G., & Shure, M. *Social adjustment of young children.* San Francisco: Jossey-Bass, 1974.

Spivack, G., & Swift, M. *Hahnemann elementary school behavior rating scale (HESB) manual.* Philadelphia: Hahnemann Medical College and Hospital, 1975.

Staub, E. The use of role playing and induction in children's learning of helping and sharing behavior. *Child Development,* 1971, *42,* 805–816.

Stokes, T. F., & Baer, D. M. An implicit technology of generalization. *Journal of Applied Behavior Analysis,* 1977, *10,* 349–368.

Stokes, T. F., Baer, D. M., & Jackson, R. L. Programming the generalization of a greeting response in four retarded children. *Journal of Applied Behavior Analysis,* 1974, *7,* 599–610.

Strain, P. S., Shores, R. E., & Timm, M. A. Effects of peer social initiations on the behavior of withdrawn pre-school children. *Journal of Applied Behavior Analysis,* 1977, *10,* 289–298.

Sutton, K. *Effects of modeled empathy and structured social class upon level of therapist displayed empathy.* Unpublished master's thesis, Syracuse University, 1970.

Toner, I. J., Moore, L. P., & Ashley, P. K. The effect of serving as a model of self-control on subsequent resistance to deviation in children. *Journal of Experimental Psychology,* 1978, *26,* 85–91.

Wahler, R. G. Setting generality: Some specific and general effects of child behavior therapy. *Journal of Applied Behavior Analysis,* 1969, *2,* 239–246.

Walker, H. M. *Problem behavior identification checklist.* Los Angeles: Western Psychological Services, 1970.

Walker, H. M. *The acting out child: Coping with classroom disruptions.* Boston: Allyn and Bacon, 1979.

Walsh, W. *The effects of conformity pressure and modeling on the attraction of hospitalized patients toward an interviewer.* Unpublished doctoral dissertation, Syracuse University, 1971.

Zimmerman, B. J., & Dialissi, F. Modeling influences on children's creative behavior. *Journal of Educational Psychology,* 1973, *65,* 127–134.

Author Index

Subject Index

About the Authors

ELLEN MCGINNIS is presently an educational consultant in the Department of Child Psychiatry, University of Iowa Hospitals and Clinics. She holds degrees in both elementary education and special education and is a Ph.D. candidate in Behavioral Disorders at the University of Iowa. Ms. McGinnis has taught in the public schools for 8 years in Minnesota, Arizona, and Iowa and has been a special education consultant in the public schools for 5 years. Ms. McGinnis divides her time among the activities of being a mother, a teacher, and a learner.

ARNOLD P. GOLDSTEIN earned his Ph.D. at Pennsylvania State University. He has worked at the University of Pittsburgh Medical School and the Veterans Administration Outpatient Research Laboratory in Washington, D.C., and has been affiliated with Syracuse University since 1963, where he is Professor of Psychology and Director of the University Center for Research on Aggression. His career-long concern, both as a researcher and clinician, has been enhancing the effectiveness of psychotherapy. Dr. Goldstein is the author or editor of 28 books and over 75 articles dealing with active therapeutic ingredients, research methods, behavior change procedures, aggression control, and the teaching of prosocial skills. His books include *Therapist—Patient Expectancies in Psychotherapy*; *Psychotherapy and the Psychology of Behavior Change*; *Psychotherapeutic Attraction*; *The Lonely Teacher*; *Police Crisis Intervention*;

Hostage; *Structured Learning Therapy*; *Skill Training for Community Living*; *Skillstreaming the Adolescent*; and *Psychological Skill Training*.

ROBERT P. SPRAFKIN earned his A.B. at Dartmouth College, his M.A. and Professional Diploma at Columbia University Teachers College, and his Ph.D. at Ohio State University. He was a member of the psychology faculty of Syracuse University from 1968–1971. Currently he directs the Day Treatment Center for the Syracuse Veterans Administration Hospital and holds academic ranks of Adjunct Associate Professor of Psychology at Syracuse University and Clinical Assistant Professor of Psychiatry at the State University of New York, Upstate Medical Center. He is co-editor of the book *Working with Police Agencies* and co-author (with Goldstein and Gershaw) of *Skill Training for Community Living: Applying Structured Learning Therapy* and *I Know What's Wrong but I Don't Know What to Do About It*. He has also authored numerous articles for professional journals dealing with psychological treatments, program evaluation, and training.

N. JANE GERSHAW earned her Ph.D. from Syracuse University. She is a clinical psychologist who has worked at Norristown State Hospital and Hahnemann Medical College and Community Mental Health Center, and she currently practices at the Syracuse Veterans Administration Mental Hygiene Clinic. She holds adjunct faculty appointments of Assistant Professor of Psychology at Syracuse University and Clinical Assistant Professor of Psychiatry at the State University of New York, Upstate Medical Center. Dr. Gershaw is engaged in the practice of psychotherapy, with special interest in therapeutic groups. She has been active in the training of professional and paraprofessional group psychotherapists and in the development of psychoeducational and group therapy techniques useful with a variety of psychiatric and nonpsychiatric populations. She is co-author, along with Drs. Sprafkin and Goldstein, of *Skill Training for Community Living* and *I Know What's Wrong but I Don't Know What to Do About It*.